The Trouble With Europe

A PLAY DESIGNED TO PUT A STOP TO THE TWENTIETH CENTURY

By Paul D'Andrea

SAMUEL FRENCH, INC.
25 West 45th Street NEW YORK 10036
7623 Sunset Boulevard HOLLYWOOD 90046
LONDON *TORONTO*

Printed in U.S.A.

ISBN 0 573 61727 9

This play is dedicated to

JOHN DENNIS

and

DANIEL FREUDENBERGER

with thanks for craft and brilliance.

The play was first produced at the Mark Taper Forum Theatre by the Center Theatre Group, Los Angeles, April 5–15, 1979. Directed by John Dennis, Set and costumes designed by Warren Travis, Lighting designed by Pamela Cooper, Music composed and sound designed by Susan Seamans Harvey.

THE TAPER CAST
(in order of appearance)

French President . . . . Hamilton Camp
American President . . . . Hamilton Camp
Inspector Jogot . . . . Bruce French
Wilbur Tilbury . . . . Jonathan Frakes
Man . . . . Benjamin Jurant
City Planner . . . . Hamilton Camp
Stewardess . . . . Kathleen Doyle
Waiter . . . . Mark Herrier
Old Man in the Tree . . . . Hamilton Camp
Girl . . . . Kathleen Doyle
Seer . . . . Kathleen Doyle
Old Man in the Underworld . . . . Hamilton Camp
Violence . . . . Benjamin Jurant
Despair . . . . Kathleen Doyle
Ideology . . . . Mark Herrier

THE PHOENIX THEATRE

Twenty-seventh Season

T. EDWARD HAMBLETON
Managing Director

DANIEL FREUDENBERGER
Artistic Director

presents

THE TROUBLE WITH EUROPE

A Play Designed to Put A Stop to the Twentieth Century

by

PAUL D'ANDREA

with

CHRISTINE BARANSKI
YUSEF BULOS
JAMES CAHILL
PERRY KING
JAMES REBHORN
KRISTOFFER TABORI

Scenery and Costumes by
MANUEL LUTGENHORST

Lighting by
DENNIS PARICHY

Movement Director
ARA FITZGERALD

Fight Director
PETER NELS

Sound by
DAVID RAPKIN

Directed by
DANIEL FREUDENBERGER

THE TROUBLE WITH EUROPE was originally produced by the Center Theatre Group of Los Angeles at the Mark Taper Forum.

January 24 - February 17, 1980

This production is made possible, in part, with public funds from the National Endowment for the Arts, a federal agency, and the New York State Council on the Arts.

THE PHOENIX CAST

(in order of appearance)

FRENCH PRESIDENT	Yusef Bulos
AMERICAN PRESIDENT	James Rebhorn
INSPECTOR JOGOT	Kristoffer Tabori
WILBUR TILBURY	Perry King
MAN	James Rebhorn
CITY PLANNER	James Cahill
STEWARDESS	Christine Baranski
WAITER	Yusef Bulos
OLD MAN IN THE TREE	James Cahill
SEER	Christine Baranski
OLD MAN IN THE UNDERWORLD	James Cahill
VIOLENCE	James Rebhorn
DESPAIR	Christine Baranski
IDEOLOGY	Yusef Bulos

ACT I

Offices of the French and American Presidents.
Airport boarding concourse.
On board a Concorde jetliner.
Air space over Paris.
Parisian café.

ACT II

The entrance to the incomplete tunnel between France and England under the English Channel.
The underworld.

PRODUCTION NOTE

Requirements:

CAST: With doubling, five men and one woman

SET: The basic set is the Underworld, a space which is partly real limestone caves underground, and partly the interior of the minds of the two travelers.

In addition to this space, fluid uses of the stage create:

the Presidents' office
airline metal detector
airliner
space
a Parisian sidewalk café

The set should be theatrical, minimalist, a space of marvels. It is not ponderous, lugubrious, or detailed. It conveys adventure, romance, comedy, gaiety, daring, charm, warmth, brio, magic.

TIME: The present

TROUBLE WITH EUROPE was nominated for Best Play by the American Theatre Critics Association, and selected as one of the Best Regional Plays.

CHARACTERS

In order of appearance:

FRENCH PRESIDENT

AMERICAN PRESIDENT

INSPECTOR JOGOT: young, handsome, arrogant, French

WILBUR TILBURY: young, daring, resolute, visionary, cowboy

MAN

CITY PLANNER

STEWARDESS

WAITER

OLD MAN IN THE TREE

GIRL

SEER

OLD MAN IN THE UNDERWORLD

VIOLENCE

DESPAIR

IDEOLOGY

Doubling arrangement:

French President; American President; City Planner; Old Man in the Tree; Old Man in the Underworld

Stewardess; Girl; Seer; Despair

Man; Violence

Waiter; Ideology

DESCRIPTIVE STORY

Modern Europe is winding down, physically and spiritually. The French and American Presidents separately send their best men to find out what is wrong with the 20th century and set it straight, in six days. The handsome, arrogant, secretly vulnerable Inspector Jogot and the visionary cowboy Wilbur Tilbury meet by accident, and start a crazy journey together. After falling out of a jetliner at thirty-six thousand feet and discussing niceties of rescue on the way down, they have a series of eccentric encounters in the criminal underworld of Paris. An aging Sibyl sends them down the abandoned tunnel between France and England, telling them that *there* they will find the trouble with Europe. The trip down the tunnel becomes a journey into their own minds. They run the gauntlet of a Frog Chorus and after fantastic adventures confront the trouble with Europe and do battle with the ills of the 20th century, saving mankind, in twelve hours. Having become friends, the two men climb out of the human subconscious toward the light and the future.

The Trouble With Europe

ACT ONE

SCENE 1

LIGHTS UP on a man standing at a desk. He has two telephones. When he is using the red telephone, he is the AMERICAN PRESIDENT. *When he is using the ivory telephone, he is the* FRENCH PRESIDENT.

FRENCH PRESIDENT. (*Picking up the telephone.*) This is the President of France. Put me through to the American President. (*Pause.*) Mr. President. Europe is winding down. We're dying here. Everything we've tried up to now has failed.

AMERICAN PRESIDENT. What precisely is the problem?

FRENCH PRESIDENT. Energy. We are running out of physical and spiritual energy. The turbines are whimpering to a halt. The holy buildings are empty.

AMERICAN PRESIDENT. I know.

FRENCH PRESIDENT. May we count on your help?

AMERICAN PRESIDENT. You've got it. You die, we die.

FRENCH PRESIDENT. We're going to put our best man on this case.

AMERICAN PRESIDENT. You know what we arranged.

FRENCH PRESIDENT. Good-bye.

AMERICAN PRESIDENT. Good-bye.

FRENCH PRESIDENT. Mr. President—

AMERICAN PRESIDENT. Yes?

FRENCH PRESIDENT. The very prayers are fading off our lips.

AMERICAN PRESIDENT. Oh. I am sorry to hear that.

FRENCH PRESIDENT. Like breath off an ice pitcher.

AMERICAN PRESIDENT. That's happening here, too.

FRENCH PRESIDENT. Our agents are fine men. They will probably be killed. Good-bye.

(*The two* PRESIDENTS *hang up.* JOGOT *enters and walks up to the* FRENCH PRESIDENT.)

FRENCH PRESIDENT. Europe is winding down.

JOGOT. I know.

FRENCH PRESIDENT. (*Powerfully.*) Your assignment is to save Europe.

JOGOT. Find the cause—

FRENCH PRESIDENT. Eliminate it—

JOGOT. And get Europe started again.

FRENCH PRESIDENT. (*Coolly.*) Correct. You have six days.

JOGOT. No problem.

(*The LIGHT on* JOGOT *goes out.* TILBURY *enters and walks to the* AMERICAN PRESIDENT. *A rough khaki backpack dangles by a strap from his left hand.*)

TILBURY. Europe is winding down.

AMERICAN PRESIDENT. You've read the reports. The frosty cocks entrusted with the dawning have stopped crowing. Seven hours after the cocks stopped crowing in Macedonia, I got word that the cocks weren't crowing in Minnesota! Minutes after there was murder for ideas in Italy, there was murder for ideas in Guyana.

TILBURY. My assignment—

AMERICAN PRESIDENT. (*Powerfully.*) Your assignment is to find the cause and get those guys going!

TILBURY. Get Europe started again.

(*The LIGHT comes up on* JOGOT. TILBURY *and the* AMERICAN PRESIDENT *are still illuminated.* TILBURY *and* JOGOT *read from their orders.*)

JOGOT. Europe is winding down.
TILBURY. The people are lost—
JOGOT. The century is old.
TILBURY. Tomorrow is mortgaged.
JOGOT. Today is sold.

(*The LIGHT on* TILBURY *goes out. The* FRENCH PRESIDENT *turns to* JOGOT.)

FRENCH PRESIDENT. What is your name?

JOGOT. I am Inspector Jogot. I am the greatest criminal detective in France. In Europe.

FRENCH PRESIDENT. What is your first name?

JOGOT. I have none. I neglected to have a boyhood.

FRENCH PRESIDENT. What do you do?

JOGOT. (*Proudly.*) I expose hidden guilt. I am the conscience of Europe. My goal is to show that every person in the West is guilty of something. I'm a hunter of men. And of women, too. They also commit a lot of crimes.

FRENCH PRESIDENT. You seem to be thorough.

JOGOT. My only regret is that there are not more laws against children. The absence of laws reduces the number of crimes they can commit and makes arrest difficult. I have to sort of wait for them to grow up. (*Complacent.*) Then I get them.

FRENCH PRESIDENT. Are you taking this assignment because you love mankind?

JOGOT. I hate mankind.

FRENCH PRESIDENT. Because you love the beauty and the artistic heritage of Europe?

JOGOT. Europe is a pudding of cash and possession. I hate beauty, loathe art, and despise artists. They are mushy swine.

FRENCH PRESIDENT. You hope women will love you if you succeed? You seek love?

JOGOT. Love is a fiction. Sex does not interest me. It is a hiccup in the groin.

FRENCH PRESIDENT. You are not moved by the beauty of women?

JOGOT. Beauty is a hookworm. It is sold for peanuts on the streetcorners.

FRENCH PRESIDENT. Why then do you intend to save Europe and the West?

JOGOT. I need lots and lots of people to accuse.

FRENCH PRESIDENT. We've done a computer study. Your chances of succeeding are zero. Your chances of being killed in the first hour of your assignment are ninety-nine in one hundred.

JOGOT. Tell your computer you are dealing with Jogot. I am no ordinary man. I am the conscience of Europe, and damn hard to kill. I am also the greatest intellect of France—

FRENCH PRESIDENT. And therefore of the West—

JOGOT. That's right, and so you can tell your computer to square root itself.

FRENCH PRESIDENT. Any identifying marks?

JOGOT. A large birthmark on my back, Excellency. Over my right shoulder blade. Some say it enhances my male beauty. All I know is, women peek at me a lot.

FRENCH PRESIDENT. Inspector Jogot, you were picked for this job because you are the best man in France. What is your class?

JOGOT. (*Proudly.*) Revolutionary.

FRENCH PRESIDENT. Your specialty?

JOGOT. (*Defiantly.*) Abstract thought.

(*The LIGHT on* JOGOT *goes out.* TILBURY *is illuminated. The* AMERICAN PRESIDENT *turns to him.*)

AMERICAN PRESIDENT. What is your name?

TILBURY. Wilbur Tilbury.

AMERICAN PRESIDENT. Occupation before government service?

TILBURY. Cowboy and truck driver.

AMERICAN PRESIDENT. What was the name of your truck?

TILBURY. Maybelline.

AMERICAN PRESIDENT. The present crisis is terrible—murder, terror, apathy, hatred—the very plants are reluctant to grow. People are lost, hopeless. Whatever it is that's destroying Europe and the West, it's dangerous and it's big. Aren't you afraid?

TILBURY. Yessir, I'm afraid.

AMERICAN PRESIDENT. Then why are you taking the assignment?

TILBURY. I kinda thought I might see something.

AMERICAN PRESIDENT. What? Come on, Tilbury.

TILBURY. (*Pushed.*) I'M NOT MAKING A LIVING WAGE! . . . Spiritually. (*Beat.*) My mind is not at rest.

AMERICAN PRESIDENT. What are you looking for?

TILBURY. A vision. I've always wanted to see a vision. Of a great city. When I drove my truck I'd get partial glimpses, through the kinetic mist—of a great city. When I rode as a cowboy, I'd get the same feeling. (*Very easygoing.*) So I'm just sort of lookin' around.

AMERICAN PRESIDENT. The fate of Europe—of the world—depends on your mission. The dynamos have stopped, Tilbury, and the holy buildings are empty. (*Pause, then businesslike.*) We have been moving toward the present emergency for five billion years. I'm giving you six days to solve the problem.

(*The LIGHT comes up on* JOGOT.)

FRENCH PRESIDENT. Did you hear that, Inspector Jogot? You've got six days.

JOGOT. I heard.

AMERICAN PRESIDENT. Tilbury, proceed immediately to the source of the trouble. How will you handle it?

TILBURY. It's a question of energy, Mr. President. I'll fly to Arabia.

AMERICAN PRESIDENT. Very well. Fly to Paris, connect with the Concorde.

TILBURY. (*Tactfully.*) Could you give me a little more time, sir? It is now five-thirty on Friday. The stores will be closed. You could have told me on Monday.

AMERICAN PRESIDENT. I was *busy* on Monday! I'm changing your orders. I want you to remedy the trouble with Europe in twenty-four hours! Do you understand?

TILBURY. I'll take care of it in twenty-four hours. (*Pause.*)

FRENCH PRESIDENT. Will six days be enough, Inspector Jogot?

JOGOT. I am the greatest detective in Europe. I have a motto: "Everybody is guilty." With such a complete list of suspects, it should be easy to find the criminal. When I find him, I will handcuff him. Six days will be sufficient.

FRENCH PRESIDENT. How will you begin?

JOGOT. Since it's an energy crisis, I'll fly to Arabia.

FRENCH PRESIDENT. Good. Take the Concorde. One more thing. The Americans have assigned their Mister Tilbury to the case. His specialty is violence. You will meet him in Arabia.

JOGOT. How will I know him?

FRENCH PRESIDENT. He always carries a khaki backpack. All of Europe awaits your success. We of France salute you.

JOGOT. Thank you, Your Excellency.

AMERICAN PRESIDENT. The French have assigned their best man to this case. Inspector Jogot. His specialty is abstract thought. You will meet him in Arabia.

TILBURY. How will I know him?

AMERICAN PRESIDENT. He has a large birthmark over his right shoulder blade.

TILBURY. How will I be able to see that, sir?

AMERICAN PRESIDENT. Twenty-four hours is a long time.

TILBURY. I'm on my way.

AMERICAN PRESIDENT. I forgot to ask—any identifying marks?

TILBURY. None that I know of.

AMERICAN PRESIDENT. Your specialty?

TILBURY. A little of this and a little of that. Nothing in particular.

AMERICAN PRESIDENT. You were chosen for this job out of one hundred million American men. You've got a specialty. What is it?

TILBURY. I've got unusually acute hearing, sir.

AMERICAN PRESIDENT. (*Masterfully.*) You can't throw me off the track. What's your specialty, Tilbury?

(TILBURY *slings his backpack by its straps over his left shoulder with his left hand. His right arm hangs at his side. He spreads the fingers of his right hand twice.*)

TILBURY. Violence, Mr. President.

(*The LIGHTS go out.*)

SCENE 2

JOGOT, TILBURY *and the* MAN *stand in front of the the metal detector at the airport.* TILBURY *carries his backpack; the* MAN *carries an attaché case.* JOGOT *is fidgeting.*

FEMALE AIRPORT ANNOUNCER. (*Through a loud-speaker.*) Flight five-oh-nine, Paris to Arabia. There will be a brief delay due to energy loss. Please wait at the metal detector.

JOGOT. Why can't we go through? I can't miss that plane.

TILBURY. The metal detector's not working. It's not lit.

JOGOT. I didn't ask you anything, mister. Keep your nose out of my business. (*A shabby* OLD MAN *shuffles up to* JOGOT.)

OLD MAN. Mister?

JOGOT. No. Whatever it is, the answer is no.

OLD MAN. I'm a city planner.

JOGOT. Get lost.

OLD MAN. (*To* TILBURY.) I'm a city planner.

TILBURY. (*Genial.*) That's a fine vocation.

OLD MAN. I know what you're thinking. I've had a run of bad luck. I knew how to make cities so they'd be fine places for people. But I've had eons of bad luck.

TILBURY. (*Pleasant and not condescending.*) You'll be on your feet in no time. Let me give you something —now this isn't a gift. It's a loan. Get you started again. Take this money and get your city planner's license renewed.

OLD MAN. It expired. When I had my troubles.

TILBURY. I'm flying to Arabia now, but when I come back you can repay me from your city planning profits, agreed? A straightforward business deal.

OLD MAN. (*With enormous reserves of insight, shrewdness and power, sounding like the* PRESIDENTS.) Agreed. You've been nice to me. Didn't have to be. It's nice to be nice. Back in the nineties, I designed the greatest of cities. (*Confidential, intense.*) Y'see, I was there, in all the great ages.

TILBURY. How about that!

OLD MAN. Oh yes. I was there. I worked on the Parthenon with Pericles. I whacked away at the Pantheon when they put *that* up in Rome. I handed Michelangelo his chisel. (*Confidentially.*) Y'know, people don't listen to me. You've been nice to me. (*Sibilant intensity.*) I designed the greatest city ever contemplated by the human imagination! (*With extraordinary power, his hand crushing into* TILBURY's *sinewy arm.*) *I have a sample!* I happen to have—a sample, here, and I'm going to give it to you.

FEMALE AIRPORT ANNOUNCER. (*Through loudspeaker.*) Passengers to Arabia, prepare to board.

OLD MAN. Hey, don't go without your sample.

TILBURY. You have a sample of an entire city? You keep it, old man. I've got to go to Arabia.

OLD MAN. (*Rummaging in his brown paper bag.*) Here. (*The* OLD MAN *removes a brick from the bag.*)

TILBURY. A brick?

JOGOT. When can we go through that thing? I can't miss that flight.

OLD MAN. Hey, don't go. Yes, a brick. A brick. It's a sample of a city.

JOGOT. It's a piece of trash. Don't pay any attention to the old fool.

OLD MAN. Watch your mouth, young feller. (*To* TILBURY.) If Europe's going to hell, you might want to build it up again.

FEMALE AIRPORT ANNOUNCER. (*Through loudspeaker.*) We are activating the metal detector. Prepare to proceed on green. (*Sound of jet engines whining up.*)

MAN. Hey, that plane's going to leave without us!

OLD MAN. Mister, it's about this brick?

(*The* STEWARDESS *rushes up, seizes the local boarding phone and addresses the little group.*)

STEWARDESS. Flight five-oh-nine, we don't have any power here. The detector's down. Just walk right through or you'll miss your flight.

(*The* STEWARDESS *walks through the nonfunctioning metal detector and boards, gesturing for the three* MEN *to follow. The* MAN *starts to go through, but* JOGOT *bars his way.*)

MAN. What *is* this?

JOGOT. You can't go through there. The detector's not working.

MAN. You heard the stewardess.

JOGOT. The stewardess is obviously an imbecile. One doesn't go through metal detectors. That goes for you, too, mister, you with the backpack there. I like to have the laws obeyed.

MAN. Who in the hell are you?

JOGOT. Be quiet. (*Jet engines whine, businesslike.*)

MAN. I'm going through.

JOGOT. (*Physically interposing himself.*) No you're not. (*Standoff.*)

MAN. I've got to make it in Arabia!

TILBURY. I sorta have to get there too, mister.

JOGOT. We wait for the detector to power up.

OLD MAN. It's about this brick— (*The* STEWARDESS *returns.*)

STEWARDESS. I told you to come on. They're closing the boarding door.

MAN. (*Plaintive.*) This guy won't let us.

STEWARDESS. Got to go. (*The* STEWARDESS *disappears into the boarding tunnel.*)

MAN. Mister, I'm going to have to get a little rough with you.

JOGOT. (*Calmly.*) You try it.

MAN. Maybe it's time to finish some people off.

JOGOT. No one's going to finish me off. I have lots of people to accuse and besides, I just bought some rental property. (*Pause.*) But I do have to get to Arabia. I *demand* that this machine power up! (JOGOT *stamps his foot and the metal detector comes alive, with its green light beckoning "walk."*) That's more like it. (*Master of ceremoniously.*) Go ahead.

(*The* MAN *balks, looks frustrated, reaches in his breast pocket for something, puts it in his attaché case, and dumps the attaché case in the trash bin. He then walks through the detector and watches the others.* TILBURY *looks around, balked.*)

TILBURY. (*Hitting upon a plan.*) Old feller, come here. I sure do like your idea of having a sample of a city.

OLD MAN. (*Evidently pleased.*) You arrange a lot of bricks just right, and you've got it, cowboy! A great city. For people.

TILBURY. Give me that brick. (*The* OLD MAN *starts to give* TILBURY *the brick. The jet engines scream.*) Now, I don't want to lose your wonderful brick—

OLD MAN. (*I-don't-want-to-cheat-you tone.*) Michelangelo chipped it a little.

TILBURY. Well, that's the way he was. Careless. Put it in here. (TILBURY *opens the backpack. The* OLD MAN *puts the brick in.*) Can you get this through that thing there?

OLD MAN. As one planner to another, yes.

(*Engines climactic.* TILBURY *hurries through the detector.* JOGOT *waits to shepherd him. Suddenly, with an athletic power, as if he were hurling the discus, the* OLD MAN *swings the backpack by its straps and lofts it over the metal detector. A deft, athletic* TILBURY *sprints and catches it.*)

OLD MAN. You'll need this!

MAN. Hey! *Hey!* If I can't, you can't!

JOGOT. Shut up! Police. I'll take care of this. (JOGOT *seizes* TILBURY *by the arm. The engines roar, nervous-making.*) I'll interrogate you on board.

TILBURY. (*Genial.*) You ought to calm down, friend.

JOGOT. I am not your friend. I am a French intellectual; and you are some kind of American idiot. The very thought of your being my friend makes me positively giddy. (*Businesslike, holding* TILBURY *by the arm.*) Come along. (JOGOT *guides* TILBURY *in the wrong direction.*) You'll have to be interrogated.

TILBURY. Okay. But . . . (*Gesturing toward the boarding tunnel.*) Arabia's *this* way.

JOGOT. Oh. I got the wrong door. Come. (*Accusingly.*) I saw that. (TILBURY *and* JOGOT *disappear down the boarding tunnel.*)

BLACKOUT

SCENE 3

TILBURY *and* JOGOT *take their seats in the jetliner, facing* DOWNSTAGE. TILBURY *has the window seat. He puts his backpack on the floor in front of him. The audience cannot see any other passengers since their seats would be directly behind those of* JOGOT *and* TILBURY.

JOGOT. Who are you?

TILBURY. Cowboy.

JOGOT. Profession?

TILBURY. Cowboy.

JOGOT. Any identifying marks?

TILBURY. None.

JOGOT. *I* have a birthmark over my right shoulder blade. Some say it enhances my male beauty. All I know is, I have quite a bit of trouble with women bothering me. Big, good-looking women. It's been this way ever since I had hair on my upper lip. Last spring I was carrying a wand of pussy willows through a giant airport. Would you believe how the women peeked at me! Just before boarding, one of them said she couldn't resist, reached out and touched the pussy willows! Do you know what I said? I said, "Please. I know. Believe me, I know how it is. But please . . . don't touch my pussy willows."

TILBURY. Good for you. And what did she do?

JOGOT. She just stopped bothering my pussy willows and *peeked* a little. You see, I never had a father, really.

(*The* STEWARDESS *appears.*)

STEWARDESS. I recommended wine. You chose wine. You chose well. Very few men in history have ever thought to listen to me. Usually they just pinch me until my thighs are numb. (*She leans over and kisses* TILBURY; *moves on.*)

TILBURY. That was a curious woman.

JOGOT. Ah, guilty. Everyone's guilty. I like guilt. I dislike children, I loathe Europe, and I particularly hate Paris. I would like nothing better than to get her entire population behind bars.

TILBURY. Isn't that a little severe?

JOGOT. You think so, but you are a cowboy and probably an idiot. I am an intellectual. I started as a butcher's boy. One day, near the university, I was trying to get my tie out of my bicycle chain. I opened the wrong door, looking for help—carrying my bicycle like this—and wandered by accident into a lecture hall. Four years later I emerged the greatest intellect of the West. I know what I want. I despise beauty, the moon and the milkweed sail. I love hunting men. And women, too. They're very guilty, too. Uh, do women usually go around kissing you?

TILBURY. Let me tell you about a woman I know back in the States—Toothy Kunstwerk. My father used to say there are three kinds of women—femina (*Said delicately.*) . . . feminini (*Said fussily and pipingly.*) . . . and feminonno. (*Said huskily and with a shaking of his right hand.*) Well, truth to tell, Toothy Kunstwerk was feminonno. I can tell you some skin-tingling tales about Toothy.

JOGOT. Wandering into that lecture hall was an accident and meeting you was an accident. I'm enjoying this.

TILBURY. Don't you want to question me about sneaking my backpack through the metal detector?

JOGOT. Oh, there's no rush.

TILBURY. But you don't understand. I want to be questioned by Inspector Jogot, the greatest detective in Europe.

(JOGOT *taps his pursed lips with his left index finger, while looking penetratingly at* TILBURY, *who stretches out in his seat.*)

JOGOT. Who are you?

TILBURY. You see, Inspector, Europe is winding down.

JOGOT. (*Looks at* TILBURY *steadily.*) We are faced with a fearful loss of energy. The cocks have stopped crowing.

TILBURY. No one knows where to go. Violence everywhere.

JOGOT. The children no longer leap. The athlete's shout—

TILBURY. The dance—

JOGOT. All die down; all are dying out, in Italy—

TILBURY. And in France.

JOGOT. Who are you?

TILBURY. A man on a mission. A cowboy taking a ride.

JOGOT. (*Decisively.*) I am Jogot of France. You must be the American, Tilbury.

TILBURY. I am.

JOGOT. We're competitors on the same mission.

TILBURY. (*Extending his hand.*) We're fellow workers. (*The* TWO MEN *smile. They shake hands.*)

JOGOT. You have no identifying marks and you are famous for your violence.

TILBURY. (*Smiles.*) That's right. How are you going to save Europe?

JOGOT. No idea. Are you fast on the gun?

TILBURY. On the draw, Inspector. We say "fast on the draw."

JOGOT. (*With a little fillip of impatience.*) Well, are you?

TILBURY. I'm nothing special drawing a gun.

JOGOT. Why did you put up with that old fool?

TILBURY. I liked him. Imagine! I got a sample of an entire city!

JOGOT. A brick! Really, Mr. Tilbury.

TILBURY. He said he was an out-of-work city planner. Lost his license. So did Toothy Kunstwerk, as a matter of fact. There's going to be a message from the Captain.

JOGOT. How do you know?

TILBURY. I have unusually acute hearing. Shhhsh.

(*From loudspeakers, "This is the Captain," and then an indistinguishable set of sounds.*)

TILBURY. It's hard to make out. Something about "uncertain weather," and "we'll have to circle."

(*The* MAN *comes down the aisle and leans belligerently over to* TILBURY.)

MAN. I saw what you did, mister, at the metal detector, and I want to tell you I don't like it. Equality!

(STEWARDESS *follows the* MAN *on.*)

STEWARDESS. A cocktail too many. Belligerent.

MAN. Shut your mouth, baby, or I'll shut it for you.

JOGOT. See here! You're a little rude! Tilbury, deal with this fellow!

TILBURY. Hey, I think you've probably got a point. Why don't you sit down in your seat and I'll come over and we'll have a talk?

MAN. (*Grabbing* TILBURY'S *tie and pulling it.*) I don't need any talk from the likes of you, mister! Understand? (*He gives* TILBURY *a shove that knocks his head against the window.*) I'm bored and I'm angry and I get *mean* when I'm bored and angry. Understand?

TILBURY. All right, friend. That's your privilege.

MAN. You bet your backpack, mister wiseguy! Equal. Equality. If *I* can't smuggle stuff on a plane *you* can't smuggle stuff on a plane. I got a mind to report you!

(*The* MAN *gives* TILBURY *another violent shove. The* STEWARDESS *tries to restrain him.*)

JOGOT. This is outrageous! Tilbury! Are you just going to sit there and *take* this?

TILBURY. (*Easygoing.*) That's what I'm going to do.

MAN. I've been balked, man! I was a poet! What did it get me? Nothing! I invented colored vowel sounds. What did it get me? Nothing! (*He strikes* TILBURY *in the face.*) Nothing. In my boredoms and in my rages I have nothing to do but strike out! (*He strikes* TILBURY *again.*)

TILBURY. (*Wiping his face.*) Look, I'm sympathetic. I had a friend who was a poet.

JOGOT. This is outrageous! (*To the* MAN.) Do you know who I am?

MAN. Shut up or I'll let you have it. I grew my hair long. What did it get me? Nothing. (*He is shaking* TILBURY *and in the process, roughing* JOGOT *up.*) I posed, I declaimed, I grew lice in my groin. (*Shaking* TILBURY *with every syllable.*) What-did-it-get-me!

TILBURY. Nothing, nothing. Say, could you take your hands off my throat?

STEWARDESS. (*Trying to restrain the* MAN.) The Captain's not going to like this. He may even become articulate over this.

MAN. So I gave poetry up! I'm in business now. I pinch the chickies! (*He gives* TILBURY *one last shove.*) I make it. (*He clutches and then releases* TILBURY. *The* MAN *is almost crying. His drunkenness is evident. Self-pity overcomes him.*)

MAN. (*Continuing.*) This whole world's going to go under, wise guy. The continents are going to crumble like crackers! Down like dogs! They threw me out! I'll smear your young men and the dancers!

STEWARDESS. Why don't we go back to our seat? I'll help you.

MAN. All right. It's just that I can't stand to see a machine cheated!

(*The* STEWARDESS *leads the* MAN *away. He is sobbing.*)

MAN. (*Continuing.*) I can't stand to see a machine cheated! The clouds will rain blood! I'll smear your young men. I'm going to blow you to kingdom come!

(TILBURY *straightens his clothes.* JOGOT *is appalled and disgusted.*)

JOGOT. Why did you let him do that?

TILBURY. I didn't let him. He just came up real fast all of a sudden and *did* it.

JOGOT. But you're trained in man-to-man, the killer pressure points, disabling techniques!

TILBURY. (*Takes his regulations book from his pocket.*) Says here: no aggressive behavior off duty.

JOGOT. Even if attacked by a belligerent drunk?

TILBURY. Says here—

JOGOT. Nonsense!

TILBURY. (*For the first time, slightly offended.*) Hey, these are genuine American regulations.

JOGOT. I say nonsense!

TILBURY. He was rumpling you. I didn't see you lashing out at any disabling pressure points.

JOGOT. My specialty, Mr. Tilbury, is abstract thought. Not brawling. Excuse me, I've got to get tidied up.

TILBURY. Same here.

JOGOT. (*Getting up, muttering.*) Inexcusable. (*Really piqued, more than he should be.*) Regulations aren't everything. (JOGOT *walks to the rear of the plane, which is elevated above their seats.* TILBURY *follows. The two* MEN *pause in front of the lavatory doors, near the large boarding door.*) How come you can hear so well?

TILBURY. When I was a baby, a snake came along and got into my cradle. My mother found it curled up by my head—apparently liked the warmth. Its tongue was flicking in and out at my ear, harmless as you please. In our part of the West, there's a folktale about a man whose hearing was marvelous because serpents licked his ears at his birth. He could hear the milkweed bleed. When I tested out hearing acute, my mother remembered the event.

JOGOT. (*His mind still on the assault; disappointed.*) Well, I'm sure you had your reasons. (*Firmly.*) Tilbury, I don't want the help of a coward. I want nothing to do with you. Stay away from me. I'll save Europe alone. (JOGOT's *hand rests on the emergency handle of the boarding door.*)

TILBURY. Jogot, you are, uh, resting your hand on the boarding door handle. The *little* door leads to the lavatory.

JOGOT. Mister Tilbury, the cocks have stopped crowing. We of the West need a rebirth. Something must be done! Something *will* be done! By me! For *I am Jogot!* I am the conscience of Europe!! (JOGOT *stamps his foot and pulls on the emergency handle. The door flies open, and* JOGOT *is sucked out into space. Screams from passengers.* TILBURY *places his hands on his hips in exasperation, turns, and runs toward his seat. Just before he reaches it, the* MAN *runs down the aisle, punches* TILBURY *in the belly, shouting, "Cheat a machine!"* TILBURY *shrugs it off and, paying no attention to the* MAN *or his action, sprints to his seat and grabs his backpack. He races back to the open boarding hatch and leaps out.*)

BLACKOUT

Scene 4

After a moment of darkness, a LIGHT REVEALS Jogot, *falling. He rotates slowly about a vertical axis. His hair streams upwards; his clothes flutter in the rush of air.*

Jogot. I never had a child. (*He continues to fall. He has reached terminal velocity and begins to enter into the process of falling to his death.*) Almighty God, protect me. (*Pause.*) I never had a child.

(Tilbury, *his rucksack streaming out behind him, swims down through space to* Jogot, *and puts his hand on* Jogot's *shoulder.*)

Tilbury. It's beautiful up here.

Jogot. (*Petulantly.*) Leave me alone. Can't you see I'm falling to my death? (Jogot *thinks for a moment.*) What are you doing here?

Tilbury. I don't know, I thought I'd try and help you out.

Jogot. (*Gettting a grip on himself and trying to be polite.*) That's really too kind of you. You shouldn't have put yourself out like this. I mean, gone to all this trouble and all—falling to your death to keep a total stranger company. It's really very nice of you. Very thoughtful.

Tilbury. (*Conversational, attempting to take the edge off a trying situation.*) The most thoughtful person I ever knew is a young woman name of Tuli Latum. It made you feel overjoyed just to be near her. She's always been like a vision to me. She has large hands— (Tilbury *and* Jogot *rotate away from each other;* Tilbury *waits until they come back into a comfortable conversational position.*) and when Tuli Latum touches things, they're grateful, even remote objects, like emirs and eldorados. They love to be touched by the chaste and delicate hand of Tuli Latum. When they are touched, they become thrones and folios and kings.

JOGOT. (*Near tears.*) This is very kind—I would like to meet her. I wish I could have helped my beloved Europe.

TILBURY. Now wait a minute. Things aren't so bad as they look.

JOGOT. (*Flashing out.*) Not so bad!— (*They rotate;* JOGOT *waits until they are head to head.*) Not so bad! The pole star staring, the moon monocular, while we plummet into the fertile soil of France! This is carrying your native optimism a bit far!

TILBURY. I happen to have brought along Clarabelle, my parachute. (TILBURY *opens his backpack and takes out a parachute which, once it is out, also streams above in the air blast.*) I'll put this on, grab ahold of you, and we'll just settle down to a gentle float.

JOGOT. I couldn't put you to the trouble.

TILBURY. Oh, it's no trouble. I'm here anyway. Come on, hold on to me.

JOGOT. (*Putting up his hand.*) No! Stop! I am an intellectual. I have principles. I refuse to be saved by a member of the middle class!

TILBURY. (*A touch of exasperation.*) Jogot, I appreciate your scruples, but critical height is approaching—wait! I'm an American! I'm from many classes! My mother chopped cotton in Louisiana!

JOGOT. So did mine! A worker! Embrace me, brother! (*The two* MEN *embrace.*)

JOGOT. (*With dignity.*) You may save me. (*Musing.*) A worker! (*While* JOGOT *muses,* TILBURY *struggles in the blast with the straps of Clarabelle, the parachute.*)

TILBURY. (*Taking the city planner's brick out of the

rucksack.) Jogot, please hold this. (JOGOT *accepts the brick and floats and rotates complacently.* TILBURY *snugs himself into the straps of Clarabelle.* JOGOT *absent-mindedly releases the brick, which plummets down along with them, appearing to float beside them in space.*)

JOGOT. We've built up tremendous energy.

TILBURY. (*Working fast.*) Here, hold this. (TILBURY *gives* JOGOT *the backpack, seizes* JOGOT, *and fingers the ripcord.*) You ready?

JOGOT. Look! The lights of Paris! They're not all out yet! I have one more condition.

TILBURY. Yes?

JOGOT. A request really. Could you set us down over there—it's a rough district but I know an excellent little sidewalk café.

TILBURY. Will do. Here we go!

JOGOT. How beautiful Paris!

(TILBURY *pulls the ripcord. Clarabelle blossoms and the two* MEN *spring heavenward. The theatre and the brick keep falling.*)

BLACKOUT

SCENE 5

Ten o'clock that night. A sidewalk café in a rough district of Paris. A tree. The WAITER *stands by a table. The table is shaded by a large umbrella.* TILBURY *and* JOGOT *fall into the chairs. The parachute settles gracefully over the umbrella, covering* TILBURY *and* JOGOT.

WAITER. I can't wait all day. I've got things to finish off.

TILBURY. Something warm.

WAITER. Two whiskeys.

JOGOT. Something light.

WAITER. Two beers.

TILBURY. Something nourishing.

WAITER. Two coffees.

JOGOT. No. Not coffee.

TILBURY. Two hot chocolates, please.

WAITER. Are you crazy? You walk in here and order hot chocolates? You're in the toughest part of Paris.

TILBURY. (*Mildly, emerging from the parachute.*) We didn't walk in, we fell in. And if you don't want to sell us two hot chocolates, we'll take our parachute elsewhere.

WAITER. (*Sounding curiously like the* MAN *on the plane.*) All right, but you'll suffer for this. We'll teach you to drink hot chocolate.

(*The* WAITER *leaves;* JOGOT *emerges.*)

TILBURY. I have never felt so threatened over a hot chocolate.

JOGOT. Waiters are a bad lot. I admire workers in general, but any given worker is somehow repulsive.

TILBURY. Do you realize that we are supposed to be saving Europe and we don't even know who or what the enemy is?

JOGOT. We'll catch a plane out of Paris for Arabia.

TILBURY. I'm not so sure that was a good idea, flying to Arabia. This violence, this murdering, this strife everywhere, this willingness to kill for slogans, is it really because energy is dying down? If so, is that energy in Arabia?

JOGOT. You're making too much fuss. I'm just going to find the guilty party and put handcuffs on him.

TILBURY. I need an insight. I need a vision. My dad used to be able to have visions. My father used to say, "Split the stick and there is Jesus." And I'd go out by the woodshed and split 'em, but all I could ever see in there was yellow-white wood, perfectly clean. Smelled good. But it was nothing but perfectly clean wood. No Jesus. Clean for a while and then it would grub up dry and dirty and die like anything else.

JOGOT. My father was a fool. Many lights winked out as we fell.

TILBURY. It will be midnight in a few hours.

JOGOT. I could see the white wings of the nuns' caps waving in the convents and the sullen prisoners inclining their heads down in the courtyards. As we fell. Penitential courtyards.

(*The* WAITER *appears.*)

WAITER. Here's your hot chocolate and I hope you're sorry. (*The* WAITER *sets the glasses down with the air of a man who has won his point.*)

TILBURY. (*To the* WAITER.) You wouldn't know anything about the trouble with Europe, would you?

WAITER. What trouble? There's nothing wrong with Europe. And even if there were, we've got the thinkers and the unions and the parties to take care of it.

TILBURY. But haven't you noticed that things are kind of dying down? Kind of a terrible loss of energy?

WAITER. Not around here they're not. We have a lot of action in this part of town. (*The* WAITER *leaves.*)

JOGOT. Is that normal? The parachute? Do all Americans carry parachutes around with them?

TILBURY. No.

JOGOT. And what was her name? The parachute's?

TILBURY. Clarabelle.

JOGOT. (*Musing over his hot chocolate.*) Clarabelle the parachute . . . You just jumped out of the plane?

TILBURY. No. I had to go back and get my backpack.

JOGOT. What's the backpack's name?

TILBURY. Anna Belle.

JOGOT. Then you weren't sucked out of the plane by the air blast from the open door?

TILBURY. (*Embarrassed, changing the subject.*) Reminds me of something that happened to Toothy Kunstwerk—

JOGOT. Never mind Miss Kunstwerk for a moment. You had to leave the door, get Clarabelle, and then come back to the open door. You just . . . jumped. Into the blackness, with Clarabelle *in* Anna Belle, after *me?*

TILBURY. The dive was risky.

JOGOT. (*Musing.*) Clarabelle *inside* Anna Belle . . . You know, I never had any real family. Mmmm. This is nice and hot.

TILBURY. (*Warming his hands on his glass.*) My father used to say, "If you dive deep enough, you will not drown."

JOGOT. My father was a fool. No one has ever cared for me. I don't care for anyone. (TILBURY *lifts his head and listens.*)

TILBURY. What's that?

JOGOT. What's what?

TILBURY. I hear something. Someone's crying softly.

JOGOT. I'll say it's softly. (TILBURY *gets up and walks around. He stops under the tree and looks up into it.*)

TILBURY. There's an old man up in this tree.

JOGOT. This cowboy is crazy.

TILBURY. And he's crying.

JOGOT. That's his problem.

TILBURY. Waiter!

(*The* WAITER *enters.*)

TILBURY. (*Continuing.*) There's an old man in this tree.

WAITER. Right. He's been there for quite a while.

TILBURY. He's crying.

WAITER. I didn't know that. He's been there for as long as I can remember. He says he has an appointment with someone.

TILBURY. In a tree?

WAITER. Right. But the someone never comes. Excuse me. (*The* WAITER *leaves.* TILBURY *peers up into the tree and says something to the* OLD MAN, *but too softly for us to hear.* TILBURY *returns to* JOGOT.)

TILBURY. The old guy in the tree says he has an appointment. He says he's waiting.

JOGOT. For whom?

TILBURY. For you.

JOGOT. He's waiting for me?

TILBURY. Right.

JOGOT. Well, I don't want to see him. Tell him to make another appointment. I don't see people in trees.

(*The* WAITER *enters.*)

WAITER. I've got a little something for you that will take your minds off your troubles.

(*Music. A* YOUNG GIRL *in peasant costume enters.*)

WAITER. What do you think?

JOGOT. Trash.

WAITER. (*Menacingly.*) I don't think you know who controls these cafés and midnight brief hotels.

JOGOT. (*Calmly.*) I know better than you. (*Menacingly.*) What *you* don't know, my friend— (*Intensely.*) is who I am!

WAITER. (*Placatingly.*) Our little girl will take good care of you. Forget about Europe. (*To the* GIRL.)

Come here. (*To* TILBURY *and* JOGOT.) This little maiden, dressed in her colorful native clothes, is really— (*He pulls the gown from her, to reveal her in the short skirt and high colored plastic boots of the street prostitute.*) a working girl. Come here. I want you to take their minds off their troubles. Sing your song. And get it right, bitch.

(*The* GIRL *smiles vacantly.*)

JOGOT. She's just a child.

WAITER. That interests you, does it? It's the effect we intend. In our business, we calculate our effects very precisely.

GIRL. (*Breaking automatically into song.*) "I'm a dainty treat."

WAITER. (*Cuffing her lightly into silence.*) Now, gentlemen, sit back and enjoy "The Song of Utter Availability." (*To the* GIRL.) Do it right, now. (*The* WAITER *leaves. The* GIRL *sings.*)

GIRL. (*Irregular and harsh.*)

"I'm available.
You can spread my legs,
You can mount my butt,
You can feel me up,
You can ramp, stamp, root and rut.
I'm available.

"I'm a dainty treat.
I'm the life divine.
I'm a light that shines.
I'm a piece of meat.
I'm available.

"For a small and shrinking sum
You can have me to the gum.
Flesh, chest, crest, cheek, neck and plum,

And then some.
I'm available.

"All is equal.
There's no sequel.
I'm sweet featured,
I'm denatured.
All is equal
I'm available.

"You can have me to the hoof.
Of my selfhood there's no proof,
So I'm available.

(*Mounting hysteria, coupled with a quality of a child pretty at a recital.*)

"If you lay in me a seed,
I've got ways to make it bleed.
I'm an economic model,
I'm a member of a class.
I'm not a maiden or a lass.
I'm a simple piece of ass!
Available!

"I'm the product of my time,
I'm just a slip-up plus some time,
So I'm available.

"My structure is deep,
My phenomena are cheap!
I have ways to make you pant.
I can make you drop your pearl.
(*With discordant scream.*)
Just don't you dare call me a woman!
And don't you dare call me a girl!"

(JOGOT *rushes forward and, in a rare display of emotion, slaps her face.*)

JOGOT. Poor creature! This would not have happened if you knew philosophy.

GIRL. All my customers are philosophers. (*She starts to sing.* JOGOT *prevents her by shaking her by the shoulders.*)

JOGOT. Barbaric catechism! Look at the steam come off her shoulders! Abraham! Abraham! I would heal you for a dukedom! What simple herb, what marjoram, would cleanse this child!

GIRL. (*Weakly.*) My phenomena—to the gum—my phenomena—

JOGOT. By St. Francis! Won't someone take this child away and wash her hands and her history?

(*The* GIRL *runs off.*)

JOGOT. God! That sickens me.

(*The* GIRL *runs back in with a stubby club.*)

JOGOT. You! You! You! You sicken me!

GIRL. The aged Thessalian said to th' Sicilian, "I can see things beyond—ach!"

JOGOT. Dowered by centuries and now a rotting copulative in his commercial grammar! You disgust me!

GIRL. My knees ache and my breasts are thick. My eyes ooze and my thighs are sick. You! You! You! This will teach your friend! (*And she attacks an unsuspecting and unresisting* TILBURY *with the club, knocking him to the ground and bloodying his head. She falls on him like a dog, growling.* JOGOT *screams. The* GIRL *runs off.* JOGOT *touches* TILBURY'S *head and then looks at his own hands.*)

JOGOT. You're all bloody! You're dripping red! It's on my hands. (*Pause.*) You really do manage to get into trouble.

TILBURY. I manage—! Jogot, you are a hot ticket. Bring Anna Belle over here.

JOGOT. (*Murmuring as he searches.*) Anna Belle, Anna Belle. (*Brightly.*) Here she is! Lighter by Clarabelle. (JOGOT *hands the backpack to* TILBURY. TILBURY *removes a first-aid kit from the backpack.*)

TILBURY. Jogot, my life's blood is staining my only working suit. I've got about nineteen hours left to find and get rid of the trouble with Europe and all I've managed to do is run around rescuing you. *Would you mind* cleaning this up? I can't get at it.

JOGOT. (*Unexpectedly kind and solicitous.*) I never really had a father, and no brother ever to help me in boyhood fistfights or to give me a boost over a fence. Here, sit down. Here. (JOGOT *gestures to the table. He helps* TILBURY, *who is a little unsteady on his legs, to the chair.* JOGOT *cheerfully pulls gauze, tape, antiseptic and other medical supplies from the kit, and sets them neatly upon the table with a brisk, professional alacrity. He peers critically at the wound.*)

JOGOT. The trouble with you is—

TILBURY. The trouble with me is I should have stayed two feet in one shoe and never left my seat in that jet airplane—which reminds me, do we get a refund?

JOGOT. For leaving in mid-air? (*A flash of indignation.*) I should think so! We didn't *use* the ticket *up!* (JOGOT *starts to feel in his pockets for his ticket.*)

TILBURY. Uh—my life's blood, remember?

JOGOT. (*Cheerful.*) Of course. Your life's blood. My, there's a lot of it! Ugly wound. The trouble with head wounds is— (*He is interrupted by a cry of pain from* TILBURY, *responding to a too violent daubing by* JOGOT *with a swab; continuing, sibilant.*) Disease! Infection drains into the brain canals, where it *rots* and becomes putrid and eats up the vital functions . . . (*Daubing vigorously.*) . . . until the victim becomes a *vegetable* . . . (*Patting soothingly.*) walking around like a tenor separated from his opera, Anna Belle, Clarabelle. *That's* the trouble with head wounds. Is this your first head wound?

TILBURY. Yes. I was always careful when I was alone.

JOGOT. I've been alone all my life. (*Cleaning, swabbing.*) When I was young I lost both my parents.

TILBURY. Sorry about that, Jogot.

JOGOT. They didn't die. I—I just *lost* them. I always misplaced things and one day they were *gone,* along with my elder brother. I didn't *know* my parents—I've always been reserved. My father's class made conversation between us impossible, and I didn't want to talk with my mother until I felt certain I could trust her—until she had proved herself through a lifetime of service to me. Then I somehow lost or misplaced them. I was five. After I mislaid them—we were catching a train, I think—I walked seventy kilometers to the cottage of an old religious aunt, our only relative. She told me my last name, screwed up her face, said "Ave Maria," and keeled over stone dead on the bright yellow tiles. I had walked seventy kilometers to meet her. I didn't know my own first name. Still don't. I was five, with mislaid parents, nothing to eat, and the smiling corpse of a religious aunt. Her cat was dead on the hot windowsill. How's that?

TILBURY. Feels very *clean.*

JOGOT. 'Tis. I made up for loneliness by making her death my first case. I decided that everyone was guilty—as indeed they are—and set out to find my parents and my brother. I am going to put the antiseptic on now.

TILBURY. Okay.

JOGOT. (*Solicitously.*) This may hurt.

TILBURY. Go ahead. If I faint, there's stuff in the kit.

JOGOT. (*Contented, chatting on.*) I thought my brother would be easy to find. He has a large birthmark on his shoulder. But I never found them. You don't have any identifying marks, do you?

TILBURY. None whatsoever. You have to be completely without identifying marks to get into our foreign service.

JOGOT. (*Absent-mindedly.*) Pity. (JOGOT *daubs in the antiseptic;* TILBURY *cries out.*) Going to faint?

TILBURY. No. I'll hang on.

JOGOT. She made a fast getaway. Uh—could I peek at your shoulder?

TILBURY. (*Slapping his hand.*) No! Will you finish repairing me? I've got a mission to accomplish. Don't you realize Europe is winding down?

JOGOT. (*Bandaging calmly.*) Women peek at me a lot.

TILBURY. (*Exasperated into affection.*) Jogot, you are a hot ticket. My dad was a drifter. He had visions. He could see things in stains.

(JOGOT *stops bandaging and waits, one hand on* TILBURY's *shoulder. Silence.*)

JOGOT. Mislaid them. Pity. (*Silence.*) Sometime you've got to tell me more about Tuli Latum.

TILBURY. Tuli had visions. As she drove her big eighteen-wheel semi. Her eyes are like wingbeats.

JOGOT. No wingbeats on that little girl who gave you this. (*Gesturing toward the head wound.*) Disgusting. A child. (JOGOT *presses the bandage.*) Hurt?

TILBURY. Feels good.

JOGOT. Fast on the gun?

TILBURY. Draw. We say draw.

JOGOT. Draw.

TILBURY. Nothing special.

JOGOT. You're a deep one. My aunt said there'd be people like you. Eyes like wingbeats? You never fight back? Well, my friend, you'll have to excuse me—I've got to save Europe.

TILBURY. Thank you. And do you have any idea of how you're going to do that?

(JOGOT *begins putting all the medical equipment back in the kit. He is thinking.*)

JOGOT. (*Meditatively.*) Europe. (*Rolling the gauze back onto its core.*) Winding down. How to . . . save it. Revolution. Scrub out the social wound, eliminate the pus, cut away the rotten flesh, cauterize if necessary, and then bandage for all you're worth . . . Revolution. Of course, that means money for posters. But who is responsible for the trouble with Europe?

OLD MAN IN TREE. Boob.

JOGOT. Now who said that?

OLD MAN IN TREE. I did.

TILBURY. It's the old guy in the tree. (TILBURY *walks to the tree and calls up to the* OLD MAN.) What do you know about the trouble with Europe?

OLD MAN. Your friend's a boob.

TILBURY. I've spent quite a bit of the night rescuing him so I can't agree with you.

JOGOT. Tell him to come down and then beat him up for me.

TILBURY. Come on down.

OLD MAN IN TREE. No.

TILBURY. Why not?

OLD MAN IN TREE. I'm afraid.

TILBURY. What are you afraid of?

OLD MAN IN TREE. I'm afraid of falling. I've been up here so long now, I'm afraid of being out of my tree.

TILBURY. Come on down. Come down and I'll tell you a story.

OLD MAN IN TREE. I don't need any stories. I already know all the stories there are.

TILBURY. I'll tell you about Toothy Kunstwerk.

OLD MAN IN TREE. I already know about Toothy Kunstwerk. You need some help. Europe's winding down.

TILBURY. Can you help us?

OLD MAN IN TREE. I don't like your friend.

TILBURY. How do you know Europe's winding down?

OLD MAN IN TREE. I have a newspaper. Says here in the paper that friendship cools. The son doesn't know the father. The smaller persons are murdered everywhere. Says here an important thinker has a fat belly. All the woodworkers have been put in asylums.

TILBURY. How can I get you to come down?

OLD MAN IN TREE. Buy a pot.

TILBURY. Let's see it. (*The* OLD MAN *throws a pot down out of the tree to* TILBURY, *who catches it.*)

JOGOT. It's trash. Don't buy it.

OLD MAN IN TREE. You need it. Buy it.

TILBURY. It's got a couple of scratches. How much do you want for it?

OLD MAN IN TREE. Your money, your wallet, and the parachute.

JOGOT. Don't do it. Without a wallet you won't know who you are.

OLD MAN IN TREE. I'm not selling to you, you boob. I've been waiting for you for years and you've never kept your appointment.

JOGOT. A genuine crazy.

TILBURY. All my money, the parachute—with ripcord and harness?

OLD MAN IN TREE. Yes.

TILBURY. The smoke canisters and streamers?

OLD MAN IN TREE. All of it.

TILBURY. My whole wallet? Cards, codes, names?

OLD MAN IN TREE. The whole thing. (*Pause.*)

JOGOT. Don't do it, Tilbury. There may be better pots down the street.

TILBURY. It's a deal. It's a lovely pot. Come on down.

(*The* OLD MAN *slowly comes out of the tree, trailing cobwebs and the leaves of many autumns after him. The* OLD MAN *clambers down, helped by* TILBURY, *and stands there in shabby vegetable disarray.*)

JOGOT. I can't believe this. Why buy a pot?

TILBURY. (*Patiently.*) When you're on a mission, you're s'posed to take advantage of any and all opportunities. Besides, I like this old guy. (*Handing* JOGOT *the pot.*) You wanta put this in Anna Belle?

JOGOT. (*Complying, shaking his head.*) I tell you it's rubbish.

OLD MAN. Now I think I can do you a service.

TILBURY. (*To* JOGOT.) See? (*Calmly to the* OLD MAN.) Can you? Why don't you sit down over here and have a cold chocolate? I really like your pot. My father loved anything well-made. He used to say, "A stitch in time—"

OLD MAN. "—is a rip in space."

TILBURY. Yeah. That's what he used to say.

OLD MAN. I'd like to help you out, young feller. You need a woman.

JOGOT. (*Grimacing.*) No we don't!

OLD MAN. You need this woman. (*Intensely, confidentially.*) Listen—Europe is winding down. Here, among the pimps and the thieves, lives an old woman—she is very frail—an old woman who sees into the mystery of things. She cannot add two and two, but being itself is her playground. (*He holds* TILBURY *and* JOGOT *spellbound with his glittering eye and his increasingly commanding presence.*) No one knows when or where or how or if she was born. No one knows whether she is a woman or a man. They say . . . (TILBURY *and* JOGOT *come in closer to hear, drawn, compelled.*) when she was a girl, male organs sprang forth while she was leaping.

TILBURY. How can we meet her?

OLD MAN. I'll bring her to you.

JOGOT. Can we go to her?

OLD MAN. She lives in these crabbed perpendicular houses away from entrances. I alone can find her. I alone can persuade her to speak with you.

JOGOT. Do you think she can help us discover what is wrong with Europe?

OLD MAN. Absolute Being is her sandbox.

TILBURY. (*Musing.*) You think she might be able to help.

OLD MAN. Her eyes are clear.

TILBURY. Go get her.

JOGOT. What can we pay you?

OLD MAN. (*Waving the wallet.*) I've been paid. (*Looks up at the parachute.*) I have always had a great fear of falling. (*He goes a few steps and stops.*) There is a problem. She is guarded by the whores and the pimps, and they are protected by the criminals. What if they bully me and refuse to let her come out?

TILBURY. (*Even, quiet, measured, calm, enormously menacing.*) You just tell them—that I am now on duty.

(*The* OLD MAN *smiles.* TILBURY *does not. He is motionless, except for his right hand, which spreads wide once and then relaxes.*)

OLD MAN. It's not easy to get her to talk. Only a handful of men ever have. She's tricky and inventive. (*He again begins to walk away, takes a few steps and stops.*) You'll have to figure out how to get her to talk. Be careful with her—no one knows how old she is. She is extremely frail. And yes, if she speaks, she'll tell one lie. Everything else will be true but there'll be one lie. There always is with prophets. (*The* OLD MAN *goes off. Silence.*)

JOGOT. An awful lot to pay for a pot.

TILBURY. My father always said, "Take what you want and pay for it."

JOGOT. (*Glumly.*) My father never said much at all. He never did anything but work. Why didn't you get him to lower his price?

TILBURY. I liked him.

JOGOT. (*Defiantly.*) Tilbury, this is utter nonsense, you're aware. Gabbling with some flea-bitten gypsy mental athlete of dubious sexuality.

TILBURY. I liked him.

JOGOT. You have bad judgment.

TILBURY. I like you.

JOGOT. (*Sulking.*) I've spit in better pots. You won't get anywhere with this, I'm warning you.

TILBURY. (*Genial, expansive, winning.*) Did I ever tell you about the time I went out with Toothy Kunstwerk? Out alone with her? A-lone? (TILBURY *sits down and* JOGOT *follows suit.*) She was a good-looking woman.

JOGOT. (*Refusing to be charmed.*) Paying all that money for a pot—and a perfectly good parachute—hardly used. Only once and even then, we used it only at the *end* of our fall. Just for a few meters.

TILBURY. Well, Toothy Kunstwerk and I, we were in the front seat when I heard this noise—

JOGOT. He's probably not going to come back with

any old woman at all. Probably out spending our money.

TILBURY. I heard this noise. Someone had stolen all four hubcaps off of Henrietta—

JOGOT. Henrietta being your car—

TILBURY. Right. All four gone as clean as you please. She's gone downhill, though.

JOGOT. Henrietta?

TILBURY. Toothy. Aged fast. I saw her just before I flew to Paris. Her beauty has settled to her chest.

JOGOT. Time is a quiet and a subtle thief. It's the very racial eye of disbelief. (*Pause.*) Time has stolen her beauty.

TILBURY. And my hubcaps.

(*The two* MEN *are still, lost in thought. The* OLD MAN *appears. He leads by the hand an aged, frail* WOMAN, *swathed in tattered clothes. She walks slowly, reluctantly.* TILBURY *and* JOGOT *rise. The two* OLD PEOPLE *come up to them.*)

OLD MAN. There was no trouble. (*He laughs.*) I told them you were on duty. This is the woman.

TILBURY. What is her name?

OLD MAN. She has no name.

JOGOT. A parachute and a pot shot! (*To* TILBURY.) She doesn't even have a name!

TILBURY. Well, neither do you.

JOGOT. (*Subsiding.*) That's a good point.

TILBURY. (*To* OLD MAN.) Are you going to help us question her?

OLD MAN. No. (*He goes to the parachute and gathers it into a bundle.*) Do you think I have nothing better to do with my time than run around saving Europe now that I'm out of that tree? I want some adventure! (*Starts to leave.*) Remember! She's very frail, and if you get her to talk at all—which practically no one has—she'll tell one lie! (*The* OLD MAN *walks off with the parachute.* JOGOT *and* TILBURY *stare at the* WOMAN.)

JOGOT. She looks like a eunuch radish.

TILBURY. Try being polite. Her teeth are perfect. I can tell she hears everything we say. (*To the old* WOMAN.) Howdy.

SEER. I didn't want to come here.

TILBURY. We need your help.

SEER. I know.

TILBURY. Our assignment—

SEER. (*Oracularly interrupting.*) My fingers can feel the edges of stains.

JOGOT. The edges of stains? Impossible. No one can feel the edge of a stain. There's no *bump*.

SEER. My eyes have been washed clean by the abundant tears that are present in everything. I strained myself in jumping and thereby came to know—everything.

JOGOT. Let me handle this. (*Assertively.*) See here, I know you're guilty of at least something. Now, you can avoid prosecution if you cooperate. How do we find and correct the trouble with Europe?

SEER. (*Spectacular oracular.*) Fly to Arabia. (JOGOT *looks smugly at* TILBURY.) There, suffer circumcision in a ceremony. You must be circumcised by angry men with their beards in their mouths.

JOGOT. (*Making mental notes.*) This is more like it. Yes. Go on.

SEER. You must cover yourself with the hide of the bull and the skin of the snake—

JOGOT. Yes—very interesting.

SEER. You must not cry out when cut.

JOGOT. Not cry—

SEER. You must fashion a shaft—

JOGOT. Yes, yes, go on. (*To* TILBURY.) Fascinating.

SEER. And rub it in a ceremonial fire-socket.

JOGOT. (*To* TILBURY.) I think we're on to something.

(TILBURY *advances on the frail* SEER.)

SEER. You must drip the warm and reeking blood of eagles— (*She is cut short as* TILBURY *grabs her by the throat with his left hand and lifts her off the ground.*)

JOGOT. What are you doing? This is a fragile but first-class seer.

TILBURY. Look, lady, I've got a little book in my pocket that says I've got to get my mission accomplished. I'm on duty. I don't buy the nonsense you're handing Jogot. (TILBURY *shakes her like a doll.*)

JOGOT. (*Horrified.*) You'll kill her! What are you doing! She's a treasure!

TILBURY. (*To the* SEER.) I want the truth from you and I want it now.

SEER. (*Choking.*) If you want it, take it and pay for it.

(TILBURY *puts her down, aims, and gives the frail* OLD WOMAN *an awesome blow to the throat. She staggers back. Determined and fast,* TILBURY *pounces on her like a big cat. He drives his fist into her belly, a follow-through blow with all the heft of his powerful body in it. She doubles up.*

JOGOT *is frantic and shouts wildly and ineffectually.* TILBURY *closes in on the bent-double* SEER. *As he comes on, she brings both hands together and up into* TILBURY'S *face. His bandaged head snaps back and he thuds to the street, landing on his shoulders and neck.*

He springs to a crouching recovery position, the fingers of his right hand on the cobblestones steadying him, but before he can clear his head, the SEER *whips her frail body forward and slams her knee into* TILBURY'S *Adam's apple. He cries out, involuntarily, in pain, a sound never heard before from* WILBUR TILBURY. *She moves in like lightning, before he can suck air into his lungs, and delivers a blow with the edge of her hand, a blow that seems to slice through* TILBURY'S *face like a knife. His head bandage loosens.*

JOGOT *steadies himself against the table in a state of shock. The* SEER *delivers a soccer-style instep kick to* TILBURY'S *stomach. The shock thuds through his body. As she sets herself for her next blow,* TILBURY *knocks her legs out from under her with a sweeping blow of his leg. She falls lightly to the ground.* TILBURY *dives on her. A kick sends him reeling.*

They meet, grapple, and she spins TILBURY *head over heels. As her dress loosens in the battle, one can catch glimpses of her delicate breasts and female thighs, which are fragrant.*

She evades a quick punch from TILBURY *and they circle each other.* TILBURY *cuffs her down, straddles her, and begins to beat her head against the cobblestones. An astonishing blow from the flat of her hand knocks the compact, athletic* TILBURY *sprawling and groggy. She leaps on his back and bites at his neck. He flips her over his head, spins her around, and fastens his massive hands on her throat. He ignores her violent, concussive kicks at his groin and slowly forces her back, squeezing her throat with the utmost of his highly trained and naturally eager resources. They hang like this.*)

SEER. (*Choking.*) I'll tell.

(TILBURY *releases her, turns his back on her, and falls to one knee, exhausted. She does not move. She is calm and unruffled, although her dress is torn and we can see her curious, delicate and beautiful breasts, like lemons on a field of snow. She is not even breathing heavily.*)

JOGOT. (*Incredulous.*) You've killed him.

(TILBURY *gets slowly to his feet. The* SEER *gracefully comes to him like a bride and takes his hand. She helps him stand. The fight seems to have eliminated seventy years from her appearance. She looks like all the women they have met.*)

SEER. You fight well. Very few men in history have ever thought to fight me. Usually they just listen. They were good. Better than you. They became immortal. But you fight well. And now you are my darling. (JOGOT *covers his mouth with his hand.*) Listen! (*She grows awesomely in power, but is without the showy oracular quality she affected earlier.*) Europe is cut off from the sources of its spiritual energy. Three demons live deep down under the minds of men. They choke it off. Below the demons lies a fantastic summa of possibility. But they choke it off. They choke off the energy. You must find and destroy the demons and liberate the energy. Men and women are cut off from the fountains of spirit. Spirit is deeper than the demons—deep, appropriate, and comely.

TILBURY. Where do we go?

JOGOT. What should I think?

TILBURY. What do we do?

SEER. Mark each word. You must go below the failed gate of communication of nations. But no one is wise enough to find the way. The roads twice diverge four times. But no one has the mathematics to understand. When baffled, penetrate. You must eat death like a salad. You will see things . . . (*Laughs.*) not quite so delicate as the feasting of dogs! You must go under the mind. Truth is trash. Die to live. Be utterly lost to find yourselves. You will succeed only if the world may be held in a pot, otherwise not. Three demons have blocked up human energy like phlegmatic clouds before the bowling and executive sun. Three demons. (*She becomes demonic.*) Only a hero can destroy the first. (*Laughs.*) No one alive can kill the second. (*More laughter, intense, cruel; a loud burst of machine gun fire.*) And no man or woman is wise enough to know how to destroy the unbeatable third. Therefore, you will perish! (*Someone can be heard humming the* GIRL'S *song. The* SEER *caresses* TILBURY'S *cheek.*) I could play with you all night, young man, and if I did, you would be versed in wonders, but you have mortal responsibilities. Arabia is a fairy tale. The trouble with Europe, my darling, (*She kisses* TILBURY.) is deep in the human mind. (*The* SEER *walks off, elegantly, gracefully, lightly, like the teacher of a dancer.* JOGOT *helps* TILBURY *to the table. They stand by the table in dazed silence.*)

JOGOT. She could have killed you! She became younger and stronger with every blow! Who would have thought to attack a fragile old woman! This is crazy! This is not realistic!

(TILBURY *moves with great effort. His chest is still heaving from his encounter with this force. But he moves to a goal. His whole attitude is one of ferocious determination.*)

TILBURY. Jogot, give me my vest from the backpack. It's on top.

(TILBURY *struggles out of his ripped coat.* JOGOT *helps him.* TILBURY *tears off his tie and throws it away.* JOGOT *hands him the simple cowboy's vest.* TILBURY *puts it on, his motions showing what the effort cost him.*)

TILBURY. Got to get going. To the failed gate of communication.

JOGOT. (*Astonished.*) You don't believe that mad-woman? She should be arrested!

TILBURY. Failed gate, man! Demons in the mind.

JOGOT. You're as crazy as she is! What reasonable man—? It's your head wound. Here, let me bandage you some more. Perhaps more antiseptic in the brain canals.

TILBURY. (*Coolly, a threat.*) Watch out, man. I'm beginning to see. The trouble with Europe is not in Arabia! The trouble with Europe is in Europe. Demons.

JOGOT. That's only metaphor! A way of speaking. Are you going out to hunt a metaphor? There are no damn demons in Europe!

TILBURY. Demons.

JOGOT. I won't let you go! If she's mad, you're a fool! If she's sane, you're dead! Remember what she said. "No one is wise enough to find the way! The roads twice diverge four times." What does that mean? What if there were demons? "No one alive can kill the second. There's no wisdom to conquer the unbeatable third." You'll perish! She's a maniac!

TILBURY. Assignment. Five out of twenty-four hours gone. Nineteen left. Save Europe. President's waiting for me.

JOGOT. (*Menacingly, while adjusting* TILBURY's *bandage.*) I won't let you go! Basta! What an imbecile!

TILBURY. The Channel tunnel.

JOGOT. What are you saying?

TILBURY. The Channel tunnel. The tunnel between France and England under the Channel. Unfinished.

JOGOT. (*Struck.*) The failed gate of communication between nations. My God! That is true. It leads—

TILBURY. Down. (*Silence.* JOGOT *revolves the possibilities unleashed by this idea.*)

JOGOT. Demons. Down. (*Without conviction.*) It's impossible. (*Working himself back up to his former state.*) No! I won't let you go.

TILBURY. Me? Us. You're coming with me.

JOGOT. Me? Off to a war no one can win against unbeatable demons under the Earth? No! I'm not going! No. Nicht. Nyet. Nein. Never. It's impossible to reason.

(TILBURY *takes a cowboy hat out of the backpack and puts it on.*)

TILBURY. That's why I need you.

JOGOT. (*Delighted.*) Me? You need me?

TILBURY. I need your languages.

JOGOT. My languages?

TILBURY. Your sophistication.

JOGOT. My sophistication.

TILBURY. And, above all, your power of abstract thought.

JOGOT. (*Calmly.*) Let's go.

(TILBURY *swings his backpack over his shoulder. The two* MEN *shake hands.*)

BLACKOUT

END OF ACT ONE

ACT TWO

SCENE 1

2 A.M. the same night. A wasteland near the Channel. Footings, posts. A series of rough arches of which one, the entrance to the tunnel, is prominent.

JOGOT *and* TILBURY *arrive, on foot.* TILBURY *is still bandaged.*

JOGOT. I won't go a step further! There are no demons in Europe! The idea! Taking a taxi from Paris all the way here to the coast. *Will you stop doing this to me!* I haven't had a minute's peace since I fell out of that airplane! I am utterly miserable. And I think I'm getting a cold. And you're so relentless! Intent! Haven't said a word since we got in that taxi. If I hadn't kept up my side of the conversation these past few hours, we'd be vegetables by now. Making *me* pay for the taxi! I *never* pay! What strange force do you possess? Is it the force of your personality? I know. You drugged the hot chocolate to make me follow you. Otherwise I, Jogot, would never do such a foolish thing as taxi to the seacoast from Paris in order to descend an uncompleted tunnel. I'm drugged, that's what I am. By Carlotta the capsule. Don't you realize you can't go down uncompleted tunnels? And pay on top of it. Merciful heaven! What crime did I commit that I should have this sky-diving, demon-driven cowboy inflicted on me? (*The one bright spot.*) At least I didn't let the driver gab all the way here. Once these cabbies get started they don't know how to stop.

(TILBURY *has been walking up and down, surveying the tunnel opening and its surroundings.*)

TILBURY. Ha.

JOGOT. (*Exasperated.*) Ha, he says. An unfinished tunnel, my idiot American friend, is the very ecstasy of an example of a blind alley. It is used in elementary textbooks. (JOGOT *notices what* TILBURY *has seen.*) Ha! Ha! Aha! There! See? A river! I told you so. It can't be done. Good. Let's call a cab and drive to Arabia. On the way we'll stop in Macedonia and have a cup of coffee.

TILBURY. Hmmm!

JOGOT. My dear Tilbury . . . (*Infinitely superior.*) my dear, dear fellow. There is a river flooding the entrance to the tunnel. If we tried to get in, we'd drown like dogs in that filthy mantling water. It's two in the morning. Think of the agony as your lungs fill up with that fetid stuff. May we go? I'll pay for the cab.

(TILBURY *sits down on a low post and pulls a pair of boots out of his backpack. He takes off his shoes and draws the boots on.* JOGOT *looks on in disbelief.*)

JOGOT. (*Quickly, with control.*) I don't want to know their names.

(TILBURY *kneels on one knee.*)

TILBURY. Hop on.

JOGOT. Hop on?

TILBURY. Hop on. Get up on my back.

JOGOT. (*Walking over to* TILBURY *and climbing on his back.*) An absurd idea. Water deep. Tilbury drown. Tilbury go on stubbornly though dead. Then Jogot drown. Europe and the West deprived of greatest intellect and nicest person. (*Fixing himself firmly on* TILBURY'S *back.*) Won't do it.

(TILBURY *gets up and wades into the river.*)

JOGOT. (*Riding, thoroughly pleased, musing, a weighing of pros and cons.*) I *can* see very well from here. That was always my trouble at parades. I could never *see,* and I had no father to give me a boost. (*The two* MEN *come to the arch.* TILBURY *stops.*) And always by the time the guilty crowd dispersed, the circus animals had absconded and dust and desert only was left. I was faced with a forlorn wasteland. The beautiful mares were gone, and the beautifully awkward clowns, with roses on their faces. (TILBURY *is immobile.*) I often try to imagine what those animals must have looked like, tracing with the mind's finger in the mind's fur.

(*A strange sound, a chorus of rasping, abrasive inhuman voices.*)

CHORUS.
Audax audax und immer audax.
Audax audax und immer audax.

(JOGOT *raises his head and sniffs the air like a stag sensing danger. One hand is raised like a paw.*)

JOGOT. What was that?

CHORUS.
Audax audax und immer audax.
Audax audax und immer audax.

JOGOT. Tilbury, I demand to know what that noise is.

CHORUS.
Audax. Audax.

TILBURY. (*Laconically.*) Frogs.

CHORUS OF FROGS.
'Dax. 'Dax. 'Dax.

JOGOT. Oh. Did you say frogs?

TILBURY. Frogs.

JOGOT. Oh. Good. (*A little happy shrug.*) Frogs is no problem. Frogs is not dangerous.

CHORUS OF FROGS.

Audax audax und immer audax.

JOGOT. I'd be happier if they'd shut out.

TILBURY. (*Mildly.*) Shut up.

JOGOT. (*Mildly.*) *They.* They're the ones. " 'Dax, 'Dax." Hidden in the pussy willows.

TILBURY. (*Mildly.*) I meant one says "shut up," not "shut out."

JOGOT. I see.

CHORUS OF FROGS.

'Dax. 'Dax. Audax.

JOGOT. (*Loudly.*) Shut up!

CHORUS.

Audax, audax.

JOGOT. Impertinent! Upstart frogs! Irrationalists!

CHORUS OF FROGS.

'Dax audax. Immerax daudax!

JOGOT. Wretched formalists! Reactionary proletarians! Lyric realists!

CHORUS OF FROGS.

Audax audax und immer audax.

JOGOT. Abstract thought doesn't work on frogs.

TILBURY. If you want to shut them up, throw something at them.

JOGOT. Very well. (*He fumbles in the backpack and takes out the pot.*) Take that! (*He throws the pot; there is a splash and the frogs are silent.*) That fixed 'em. I'll teach them to audax me. If there's one thing I cannot stand, it's an impertinent frog. I've cleared the way. Tilbury, push on!

(TILBURY *walks through the arch. He is now on firm ground. He kneels and* JOGOT *gets off.* TILBURY *takes the backpack from* JOGOT *and takes a flash-*

light out of it. He gestures toward the interior of the tunnel.)

TILBURY. Come. This way.

JOGOT. "This way." How many ways are there in a tunnel? (*They walk into a maze of half-built arches roofed with vaulting.*) What kind of seer would neglect to mention a legion of frogs guarding the gateway? (*They continue to walk.*) Disgusting. That's what she was. A child and bewhored. Makes you feel like quitting the human race.

TILBURY. She bit me.

JOGOT. When she fell on you? Where did she bite you?

TILBURY. It's a little embarrassing.

JOGOT. Where?

TILBURY. She bit me on the nipple.

JOGOT. (*Wincing.*) Oooh. That must hurt.

TILBURY. It hurt. Still hurts.

JOGOT. I should have bandaged it.

TILBURY. It was a mean thing to do. (*They walk.*) Reminds me. Did I ever tell you how Toothy Kunstwerk got her start? You there?

JOGOT. Right here.

TILBURY. One day a friend of hers discovered she actually possessed new car smell. Naturally. It was part of her. He advised her to market it. Well, there was no stopping a product like that. Toothy went right to the top.

(*The two* MEN *walk on.*)

JOGOT. (*Trying to appear merely conversational but enjoying it all immensely.*) I was fascinated to hear of Tuli Latum's visions as she drove on the great roads. Right now, in my mind's eye, I can see her blasting across the American highway in the luminous pre-dawn purple, her long legs astride a thousand chromium horsepower.

(*This drags* TILBURY *out of his professional concentration.*)

TILBURY. (*Pausing, putting one boot up on a rock.*) My goodness she is a beautiful woman! Y'see, I've known Tuli since she first started filling out her jeans.

JOGOT. Go on.

TILBURY. We'd better—Did I—uh—ever happen to describe to you her breasts?

JOGOT. (*With restraint.*) Why, no, Tilbury. I don't believe you ever did.

TILBURY. Don't get her wrong now. She's a chaste and modest girl. But active. She's almost always in motion—swinging that long leg like a lasso up over a horse, or swishing three hundred and sixty degrees of horizon up into her bright hair, or getting on down under the semi to check on a brake line—you kind of get a glimpse now and then—blouses being what they are—even if you're not trying to—even if she's not trying to—even if *no* one's trying to, blouses are what they are and breasts are what *they* are and where they are—and willy-nilly, life being what *it* is, you get a glimpse now and then—of other worlds. (*Silence.*) You're kind of quiet. You want to get on with our mission?

JOGOT. (*Too calmly.*) A brief discussion of Tuli Latum's breasts would not be inappropriate at this point in the tunnel. Europe can wait a minute or two.

TILBURY. Close your eyes, Jogot, and imagine to yourself milk—

JOGOT. Milk.

TILBURY. Not a vessel of milk, but milk itself, the pure abstract white globe of the thing in itself. Now—have you got the milk in your mind?

JOGOT. Yes, I do. I'm very good at this sort of thing.

TILBURY. Now imagine its perfect and spatially limitless globedness folding back in on itself. Twice.

JOGOT. Yes.

TILBURY. Have you got that?

JOGOT. Yes.

TILBURY. Twice. Now picture the delicate film that covers milk when you heat it ever so carefully. Can you see it? That delicate film?

JOGOT. Yes, I can. Delicate. Delicate indeed. My, but it's delicate.

TILBURY. Now imagine that weight previously envisioned, supported and contained only by that delicate film-skin, *almost* bursting, suspended, but not quite bursting—all held in on itself by that delicate film. If you were to touch it—

JOGOT. My God! It would burst immensely!

TILBURY. (*Heaves a sigh.*) You've got it. (*Silence.*) Well, what do you think? Back to Europe?

JOGOT. You've never touched Tuli?

TILBURY. No.

JOGOT. She loves you?

TILBURY. Tuli has an extraordinary mind. She thinks things out the way a meadow would—green, completely, with detailed attention to motes and birdcalls.

JOGOT. So?

TILBURY. You asked me if she loves me. She shouldn't, being as smart as she is, but I think she does.

(JOGOT *muses. The two* MEN *walk on.*)

JOGOT. She makes me feel like a fool. On the plane —silly.

TILBURY. What? Open the boarding door of a jet at thirty-six thousand feet? Silly? Don't be hard on yourself, Jogot.

JOGOT. Precisely. I was a fool. As I fell, I saw the steady, unfalling moon. I felt love for the moon, while my hair streamed like a comet and the friendly air blasted up at me. You have no idea what it's like—falling.

TILBURY. I was falling, too.

JOGOT. But you knew what you were doing. I didn't. There's a big difference. I suddenly realized that I have never loved anyone and that I have no child. I, Jogot! The greatest intellect of the West. Then you happened by.

TILBURY. Happened by! Jogot, you are a hot ticket. Oh. (TILBURY's *hand explores the blank wall of the end of the tunnel.*)

JOGOT. (*Primly.*) I told you so. ItoldyousoItoldyou-so! I just want to say I told you so. Let's go back. There's no question now but we've *got* to go back. There'll be time for a little nip of something, a nap, and on to Arabia. An utterly blank wall. Millions of tons of stuff in the way. Journey impossible. Jogot vindicated.

TILBURY. Whoa. Now hold on. The seer said, "When baffled penetrate." We're baffled, all right—and what's this? (TILBURY *shines his light on a rusted shaft-like mass propped against the wall.*)

TILBURY. A jackhammer.

JOGOT. Left behind.

TILBURY. By the workers.

(*The two* MEN *think of the same thing.*)

JOGOT. Tilbury, if by any remote and impossible chance you intend to *use* that jackhammer to—

TILBURY. Penetrate when baffled—

JOGOT. You should know that (a) it is broken, (b) it is rusty, (c) it is old, (d) it is not *your* jackhammer, (e) it won't work, (f) if it did, all you would do is pour the Channel down on our heads—ecchhh! Death by drowning—and I already have sniffles—'course it would also get those damn frogs! —'course they can swim and they're small— (l,m,n,o,p) it is im*prob*able and (x,y,z) we're crazy to be here and if anyone finds out . . . (*Sigh of relief.*) besidesIsee there'snospark-plugheehee. No spark plug.

(TILBURY, *silent and implacable, swings his backpack down.* JOGOT *looks on in horror as* TILBURY *removes . . .*)

TILBURY. Sally Jo, my emergency spark plug.

JOGOT. Sally Jo—his spark plug. Is this *normal* behavior for Americans? (*Dying hope.*) Wrong size? (TILBURY *starts to fit the plug.*) Wrong thread? Wrong color?

(TILBURY *does not answer. He tightens Sally Jo in with Michele, the plug wrench. He rubs the renovated jackhammer with his sleeve, and tugs at the starter rope. Nothing happens.*)

JOGOT. It's rusted tight, out of fuel, outmoded, you don't have a license, you're probably breaking union rules—I'm not asking for out and out socialism, my dear Tilbury, but I would think you'd have a feeling for union rules—it's after hours, we're supposed to be saving Europe, for heaven's sake. I haven't had a thing to eat and I think I'm going to cry. It's not a pretty sight.

(*Silent, resolute,* TILBURY *bashes the apparatus with his foot. Nothing happens.* TILBURY *hunkers down and touches the rusty and abandoned jackhammer with the tenderness only powerful and violent men are capable of.*)

TILBURY. Sweet, what's the matter? Now, now. No name? Feel like you're nobody? Come, come, Susannah.

(*He gently pulls the starter rope and Susannah, the jackhammer, chatters into life. No one can hear anything above the insistent clamor of Susannah, although* JOGOT *is saying a great deal.* TILBURY *blasts away at the base of the tunnel wall for a minute and then turns the machine off.*)

TILBURY. Won't break through.

JOGOT. You madman! Do you realize how many tons of water are poised above our heads? What if your abominable jackhammering tore down the ceiling? I won't put up with this, do you hear? I won't be lugged around like a sheep tick by you and your all-girl band. I've got work to do. I've got people to accuse. I've got scads of hidden guilt to find. I've got to correct the trouble with Europe in six days and I've already shot eight hours. I demand you carry me out of here! I am Jogot! The conscience of Europe! (JOGOT *stamps his foot in rage. All is silent.* TILBURY *listens. He quickly picks up his backpack, dusts himself, and stands ready.*)

TILBURY. Jogot, you are a hot ticket. I think you did it.

(*Rumbling. Suddenly the floor falls out from underneath the two* MEN. *They disappear into the chasm. Dust, uproar, and then silence.*)

SCENE 2

A LIGHT ON the two bodies falling, high UPSTAGE. The wind whiffs past the two tumbling forms. Four seconds. LIGHTS OUT.

SCENE 3

The scene is the underworld. Desolate, labyrinthine, etched by time. Arches, passageways formed by erosion, tenebrous glooms. Groans as TILBURY *and* JOGOT *come down. LIGHT COMES ON just as they land in a shower of rubble. The two* MEN *get up.*

TILBURY. Are you all right?

JOGOT. (*Dusting himself off, trying to preserve his dignity.*) I am. No, leave me alone, I'm perfectly fine.

TILBURY. We penetrated. Thanks to you.

JOGOT. Penetrated! Nonsense. If anyone ever learns of this—

TILBURY. We're doing just what the old woman said we should do. Come on.

JOGOT. Where?

TILBURY. On.

JOGOT. (*Aged wisdom speaking to a child.*) Tilbury, let me try to reason with you. I'm on a mission. You're on a mission. You're a charming fellow, but we're *not* going to find the trouble with Europe in any underworld, metaphorical or otherwise. I've got to get on my plane. I've got to catch the two-thirty frog out of here.

TILBURY. (*Genially.*) Come *on,* Jogot.

JOGOT. (*Starting to move on, following* TILBURY.) At the *latest* the three-fifteen avalanche.

(*A sound, as of a large stone falling into water.*)

JOGOT. (*Imperiously, holding* TILBURY *responsible.*) And what was that?

TILBURY. (*Thoughtfully.*) I don't know. These caves must be limestone hollowings. Water eats the softer stone away. That noise must be deposits falling into an underground river or lake. Come on. (*Soberly.*) She said that after we passed the threshold we'd see something that would not completely please us, something not quite so delicate as the feasting of dogs. Come on.

JOGOT. Oh, all right, but if I get killed you'll be sorry you did this to me.

TILBURY. I did this to you? Who opened the boarding door of the plane? Who stamped his foot? (*Mimicking.*) "I am Jogot, the conscience of Europe"? (*He stamps his foot.*)

JOGOT. (*With great respect for his own powers.*) Careful.

TILBURY. Don't worry, it doesn't work when I do it. You're at least as responsible as anyone.

(*They walk under the arches, through the convolutions of the underworld. The sound of something falling into the water.*)

JOGOT. I don't like those sounds. (TILBURY *stops.*) Why are you stopping?

TILBURY. Trouble.

JOGOT. Trouble. Practical?

TILBURY. Tactical.

JOGOT. In particular?

TILBURY. Directional.

JOGOT. Howso?

TILBURY. Fork in the road.

JOGOT. Which way do we go?

TILBURY. Don't know.

JOGOT. (*Flashing out in impatience.*) Figure it out. Deal with it, Tilbury.

TILBURY. You're acting as if you think we are on to something.

JOGOT. (*Completely seriously.*) We are. Do *do* something. Oh, I hate it when people dilly-dally, dawdle, and delay. Come on. Think of something. You're fast on the gun.

TILBURY. We say "fast on the draw."

JOGOT. Come on! I can't stand idlers!

TILBURY. (*Shrewdly.*) Which way would *you* say we should go?

JOGOT. (*Decisively.*) Left!

TILBURY. (*Equally decisively.*) Good then. It's settled. When you opened the door of the jetliner, you really wanted to wash your hands?

JOGOT. Right! My fingers were sticky from the cookies!

TILBURY. But you opened the hatch. And when we were falling over Paris, you meant to put the brick back in the backpack, but you dropped it?

JOGOT. Right! The brick was trash anyway and I was half a pirouette from death.

TILBURY. And you thought the pot was a stone and threw it at the frogs?

JOGOT. Right!

TILBURY. And you're the greatest thinker in Europe?

JOGOT. I am.

TILBURY. And here at the fork you say left?

JOGOT. Left!

TILBURY. Then we go right.

JOGOT. Now I *am* insulted. I, Jogot—

TILBURY. Shush. Don't go stamping around. We're already at the proper level. Let's go.

(*They disappear down the right-hand passageway.*)

SCENE 4

The two MEN *reappear from under one of the arches, as they traverse the dark interior. They weave in and out of the convolutions of the underworld.* TILBURY *stops and* JOGOT *runs into his back.*

TILBURY. (*Turning his flashlight away.*) You won't want to see this.

JOGOT. What?

TILBURY. Inspector Jogot, there are three—bodies—here, of young women. They have been rather badly—mutilated. (*His hand wanders vaguely to his mouth.*) You—won't want to see it.

JOGOT. I must. (JOGOT *takes the flashlight and shines it on the bodies, which are hidden from the view of the audience. He looks and winces with revulsion.*) I am ashamed I am a man. (*The two* MEN *look at the dead bodies;* JOGOT *crosses himself unconsciously.*) Who could have done such a thing?

TILBURY. Any of us.

JOGOT. They were extremely beautiful. The mutilation stands out in bold relief against the beauty.

TILBURY. They've been firebombed. Or napalmed. Or something.

JOGOT. You can see that the attack was well thought out. Who else has been down this tunnel?

TILBURY. All of mankind.

JOGOT. Impossible. I've never read any reports of people being down here before.

TILBURY. Jogot, someone's been down here before.

JOGOT. (*Looking at the bodies.*) Yes. Something's growing in me. I've always thought love was lust. But I wish someone could have given these beauties—love. One has her face turned away. Should we look at her face?

TILBURY. No.

JOGOT. Because it is probably also mutilated?

TILBURY. No. It's not part of the vision. Leave her as she is. We are not supposed to know what happened to her face. Leave her in peace now. Come. Come, Jogot. Leave this terrible thing behind.

(*The two* MEN *walk on.* JOGOT *glances back over his shoulder.*)

JOGOT. It's unreal. (*They take a few steps.*) But what could be more real than those bodies? Let's push on. But if the old woman was right, we're going to encounter the trouble with Europe and perish. Only a hero can face the first of three demons, no one alive can destroy the second, and no one is wise enough to kill the matchless third. If she's right, we're dead, whereas—

TILBURY. Trapped underground as we are, and getting more lost with every turn—

JOGOT. If she's wrong—

TILBURY. We're dead.

(*They walk,* TILBURY *leading.*)

JOGOT. Dead right, dead wrong. A tough equation.

(TILBURY *stops, and* JOGOT *runs into his back.*)

JOGOT. Why are you stopping?

TILBURY. Trouble.

JOGOT. Trouble. Practical?

TILBURY. Technical.

JOGOT. In particular?

TILBURY. Navigational.

JOGOT. (*Quiet pride.*) I believe I can be of help. Ask me the way.

TILBURY. This time it's insolubly complex. There are three roads.

JOGOT. Oh. One honest blunder wouldn't be enough then, would it? Even I am useless here! A genuine mathematical quandary.

TILBURY. And no instructions from the seer.

JOGOT. (*Briskly.*) All right! Come on now! Chin up! (*Complacently, confidently.*) What do we do, Tilbury?

TILBURY. Let me explore each one. You stay here as a reference point.

JOGOT. My idea exactly. I stay here.

(*The LIGHT dies down as* TILBURY *disappears into one of the channels, comes back up as he reappears, and then dies down again as he explores the next channel. It is dark.*)

JOGOT. Thank you, Tilbury. It's very kind of you to touch me reassuringly, here in the darkness. You're the kind of truly virile man who simply is not afraid of showing affection, who is not afraid that the world will misinterpret a simple act. I like you, too, Tilbury. But why are you touching me simply and affectionately *on the ankle?*

TILBURY. Well, I like you, too, Jogot, but I'm over here.

JOGOT. Don't be silly. There's a hand grabbing my ankle. Logic clearly implies—

TILBURY. Right. But logic or not, I'm about twenty meters away from you, over here, and I have short arms.

JOGOT. Tilbury! Come here im*med*iately and tell me who or what is clutching my ankle. I find it very unprofessional to have my ankle clutched by a total stranger in the underworld. I'm on duty and it is an act which is awkward in itself.

(TILBURY *walks to* JOGOT *and in the illumination cast by the flashlight the two* MEN *can see an* OLD MAN, *half-buried in stone and earth, his face and beard whitened with rock dust. He is clutching* JOGOT's *ankle.*)

TILBURY. He's half-dead.

JOGOT. Who-are-you-what-are-you-doing-here-who-are-you-leavemealone.

TILBURY. He's probably a worker from the tunnel project who got lost. He's really pinned to the rock.

JOGOT. The poor man! Dig him out, Tilbury! (*And, amazingly for* JOGOT.) In fact, let's both dig him out!

(TILBURY *and* JOGOT *set to work removing the rocks and other debris from the* OLD MAN. JOGOT *takes* TILBURY'S *kerchief, wets it in the river, and gently wipes the* OLD MAN'S *face. Once his face is clean, the* OLD MAN *resembles the* CITY PLANNER, *the arboreal* OLD MAN, *and* JOGOT.)

JOGOT. He's half-dead!

TILBURY. He's got something in his hand.

JOGOT. More trash. Throw it away.

TILBURY. (*Trying to pry the object loose.*) He's not letting go. He's got the grip of thirty men. Moisten his lips. Maybe he can talk.

(JOGOT *moistens the* OLD MAN'S *lips tenderly.*)

JOGOT. He's trying to speak.

OLD MAN. (*His voice sounds like the* PRESIDENTS'.) You're late. (JOGOT *and* TILBURY *look at each other in amazement.*) You're late. I've been waiting for you for centuries. Can't you hear it? (*They listen.*) Can't you hear the silence of the cocks? Pick me up. (JOGOT *and* TILBURY *pick up the* OLD MAN *and support him between them.*) It's that way. (*He points to the center channel.*)

JOGOT. (*To* TILBURY, *awkwardly past the* OLD MAN.) Who is he?

OLD MAN. (*Imperiously.*) It's always the same. One quiet one and one fool. (*To* JOGOT.) You. Be still. (*To both.*) That way. We go to our deaths.

(*The three* MEN *disappear into the center channel.*)

SCENE 5

The three MEN *appear as they come out of one of the infinite number of winding passages in the limestone underworld. The* OLD MAN *is supported between* JOGOT *and* TILBURY. *As the three walk on, extraordinary shapes, luminous, spectral, and reminiscent, float by in the darkness.*

JOGOT. (*In a loud whisper.*) Tilbury! Are you there?

TILBURY. Yes.

JOGOT. Tilbury! I'm fantasizing. I'm going crazy. I didn't bargain for this. I don't want this old fellow to hear, but he's right between us. If you can hear, he can hear.

TILBURY. (*Whisper.*) So speak in a normal tone.

JOGOT. (*Whisper.*) All right. (*Normal.*) All right. Look, I'm breaking up under the strain. If you get out of this alive, tell them at headquarters that my mind started going a little after four in the morning, but that I carried on as best I could. Would you tell them that?

TILBURY. Sure, Jogot, but we're both going to make it. (*Silence.*)

JOGOT. Tilbury! You there?

TILBURY. Yes.

JOGOT. Who, uh, who do you think you-know-who is?

TILBURY. Who?

JOGOT. *You know who!* Stuck in a limestone deathtrap with an impudent cowboy and a bossy fossil. Hey, Tilbury, my mind, as previously alleged, is going.

TILBURY. (*Grunting with the effort; he is carrying most of the* OLD MAN's *weight.*) What makes you think so?

JOGOT. Apparitions. I'm seeing apparitions—

TILBURY. Fantastic shapes—

JOGOT. Luminous monstrosities—

TILBURY. All colors—

JOGOT. The exhalations of dragons—

TILBURY. The combs of igneous cocks—

JOGOT. Scarlet octosyllables—

TILBURY. A tribe of peacocks fed exclusively on hand grenades—

JOGOT. You see them, too?

TILBURY. Yes. I think we are looking—

JOGOT. Straight into our own minds.

TILBURY. That's right, partner.

JOGOT. This can't be happening to me.

OLD MAN. Silence! Put me down. You are about to eat death like a salad. I am the residual man, the one who remembers. I have lived in the underworld of the human consciousness, ignored, waiting century after century for heroes to trek down here. You two are the first to come since the conqueror. You are fine boys. You will probably be killed. Here in the underworld of the human spirit live the demons that are suffocating Europe!

JOGOT. I am a modern man and proud of it. One thing we know today is that there are no demons.

OLD MAN. Look about you.

(*Walking toward them is* DEMON VIOLENCE, *with a half-human turret upper body supporting two cannon-like arms, which terminate in red-lensed laser-like spotlights. Its eyes are twice as wide open as they should be. Its mask-like face is hysterical. Its skin, if touched, has the sticky quality of blood just before it is dry.*)

JOGOT. Oh, my God, what is it!

OLD MAN. There stands Political Violence. Before he was ripe he was rotten into murder. He sends the rocket across the border into the child's throat. No one has ever listened to me. He sets the torch to the village and murders the alien who is his secret brother with different lips. I am dying. I am old. I have waited for you for centuries. (*Rebuke.*) You and your grandfathers are late, late!

JOGOT. It's going to see us.

OLD MAN. These demons intercept the forces of life that make the child leap and the silk of the milkweed sail. It's seen us!

(*The flesh of the* MEN *seems fragile before the metallic competence and cruelty of* VIOLENCE. *Its powerful voice has an electronic resonance, like a human voice amplified by hundreds of watts.*)

VIOLENCE. Who faces me? Why are you here? Could you not wait to be killed in your turn, but you must come to me ahead of time in my dwelling?

(JOGOT *stares in disbelief.* TILBURY *reaches into his backpack and takes out his gunbelt, holster and six-shooter. Red light pours out of the cannon of* VIOLENCE. TILBURY *slowly and deliberately buckles on his belt and ties the holster thong to his thigh. He checks the chamber of his revolver and thuds the gun into its holster. He wears the gun high, its handle at hip-level.* VIOLENCE *boasts his hero's boasts.*)

VIOLENCE. I have made blood pudding of your continents. In your pools of the countryside I have ringed the reeds black with blood. What man dare face my terrible celerity of purpose? I strike irresistible like the strafing run, a terrible noise out of an empty heaven, so powerful in armament and jet ecstasy that not even the boldest child can stop me, no, not even the old spinners of cloth. (*Laughter from* VIOLENCE.) I lick from my fingers the smeared young manhood of nations!

(*The powerful red-lensed spotlights traverse the wings and then the audience as the beams come together like a pincer to crush* TILBURY, *who stands arms at his sides, booted and pistolled, head bandaged, cowboy hat cocked to one side, in front of the* OLD MAN *and* JOGOT. JOGOT *has dropped to one knee. As the rays near him,* TILBURY *makes his hero's boast.*)

TILBURY. I am Tilbury of the American West. I trained for you in trucks and trenches. I fear no demons. Serpents licked my ears at birth. My hand moves like the rattler striking.

(VIOLENCE *begins to fire rays of light that explode in giant splashes of red and yellow like powerful spotlights being flashed on and off.* JOGOT *falls to the floor of the cave.* TILBURY *dodges behind the stalagmites of the underworld, firing when he can. The battle rages. Then, suddenly,* TILBURY *emerges with his gun in its holster.* VIOLENCE *turns like a turret to finish him when* TILBURY *draws with invisible speed and fires three shots like the rattler striking. The lights and turret of* VIOLENCE *explode. Silence. The demon shudders and then topples with a terrific crash.* TILBURY'S *shoulders sag. The* OLD MAN *is unconscious.*)

JOGOT. (*Incredulous.*) The thing is dead. We can't lose. Fire power. All right, so there are demons down below. Granted. Fire power! Send Tilbury in!

(*Threading its way down the underworld passages comes* DEMON DESPAIR, *a smallish android figure in a skintight metallic suit, wearing the high yellow plastic boots of the* GIRL *at the café.*)

JOGOT. This one doesn't look so tough.

DESPAIR. Come here.

JOGOT. Is it a man or a woman?

DESPAIR. Come.

JOGOT. I think it's a man.

TILBURY. I think it's a woman.

JOGOT. I tell you, she doesn't look so tough. We'll just beat her up. The other one had a turret and everything. You kick her in the belly and I'll pull her hair. Go grab her. I'll bite her on the nipple.

DESPAIR. I saw your display of power. You probably could annihilate me with one blow. Come. A little closer. (*Sense of discovery.*) You're *men,* aren't you?

JOGOT. We are. And who are you?

DESPAIR. I live . . . down here in the mind. (*Beat.*) Say, I don't want you people to hurt me, because I'm weak and I bruise easily.

(DESPAIR *approaches* TILBURY.)

TILBURY. (*Holding up his gun.*) You hold it right there or I'll blast you.

DESPAIR. All right. I saw what you can do. That's never happened here before. You're a powerful guy. But your hands . . . are stained with blood. I c'n sorta smell it. (*To* JOGOT.) I know you. You've put your intellect to obscene purposes in philosophy and the other works of greed.

JOGOT. You're mad.

DESPAIR. Nope. You have. There's blood on your hands too. People kill for your ideas.

TILBURY. Look, I've killed one demon and I can do the same for you.

DESPAIR. What makes you think I'm a demon? What're you, crazy? Huh? (*To* JOGOT.) Who's your friend? You oughtta straighten him out.

JOGOT. Who or what are you?

DESPAIR. I dunno. I just live down here in the mind. I guess I'm a neuron or somepin'. I just hang out down here.

TILBURY. Jogot, I think I ought to blast this one just for safe keeping.

JOGOT. Hold on. She intrigues me. (*To* DESPAIR.) What are you?

DESPAIR. I can't hurt you. Come a little closer to me. Both of you. It's really something that you two are down here. I mean, never before. Usually I have to go up there and get them.

(TILBURY *looks at* JOGOT.)

TILBURY. The old woman said three demons.

DESPAIR. I'm no danger to you. Unless— (*Turning on them with a bewildering moral intensity.*) Aren't you the ones who killed those girls back there?

JOGOT. You're crazy. We didn't do that.

DESPAIR. I'm afraid you're not thinking very clearly, Inspector. They're in your mind, aren't they? (*Circling them.*) You're modern men. Knowledgeable. That's the way I like 'em. I'll bet you know that love is a hiccup in the groin. You pocket the poor and market the whore. (TILBURY *levels his gun at* DESPAIR.) Oh, I don't think you're going to do that. Those things don't work on me. I'm going to give you two a real treat. It's kind of a peep show. All I want you to do is to look into my eyes. I don't know if you've noticed it, but I'm in your mind. And looking into your mind is your kind of thing, Inspector, right?

JOGOT. Right. Let me handle this, Tilbury. I'll look. I'm not afraid of looking at anything. That's my specialty. (JOGOT *approaches* DESPAIR. DESPAIR *lifts her head and* JOGOT *looks into the heart of darkness.* JOGOT *reels back.*)

DESPAIR. (*To* JOGOT.) Now tell your friend what you saw.

JOGOT. I saw . . . my thoughts as I fell from that plane.

DESPAIR. Say them out loud.

JOGOT. No one should know that.

DESPAIR. Say them out loud for the rest of your mind to hear.

JOGOT. No!

DESPAIR. You must.

JOGOT. (*Compelled by the force of what he has just seen.*) I saw . . . emptiness. When I fell from the plane I realized as fast as the sheet lightning billowing out from the pole that I was utterly empty. The sum total of my life of abstract thought was that I believe in nothing and I have no child. I worship nothing—

DESPAIR. And so you worship *me.*

JOGOT. (*Stunned.*) I do. Who are you?

DESPAIR. I am the center of your century. Now, Inspector Jogot, what do you think your friend here should do?

JOGOT. (*To* TILBURY.) You should look into its eyes.

TILBURY. (*Hesitating.*) Jogot? Old buddy?

JOGOT. Yes. Yes.

DESPAIR. Come.

(TILBURY *approaches, and looks.* TILBURY *slips his gun into its holster, and walks to an outcropping of rock, and sits down dejectedly.*)

TILBURY. Jogot, I never told you how Toothy Kunstwerk ended up. It was an ugly business. The details were unclear. A woman dead and a child-suicide. The legal details were unclear. It died out of the papers.

JOGOT. I think of that girl at the café.

DESPAIR. I've always said, I'm worth looking at. Why don't you two go on now back up and tell the others what it's all about.

(*The* OLD MAN *stirs.*)

OLD MAN. Don't look at her. She'll make you want to die.

DESPAIR. (*Preening.*) But my eyes, my thighs, my merchandise.

OLD MAN. Look instead at this piece of clay I've saved for twenty thousand years.

DESPAIR. It's trash. Don't take your eyes from me.

OLD MAN. This piece of clay has patterns shaped by human hands of great antiquity. It's been beaten on by a human heart. I can read it.

DESPAIR. Don't take your eyes from my eyes.

OLD MAN. Here are the forms of barley, and millet—

JOGOT. And these?

OLD MAN. Those signs represent the burst-pomegranate waters of the Mediterranean. Here is amber inlay, showing knowledge of magic in the maker—

DESPAIR. You must look at me. I need your worship, your gaze. Think of my legs among the cigarettes.

OLD MAN. These grains freed men from need-bondage. Hands fed by female gardens played and made.

JOGOT. Here are the signs of chiefs and war—

OLD MAN. But with them came the gifts of art. Men with angel intellects became numerate and literate, and washed their ankles in the Milky Way, recording what they found *here*—

TILBURY. The code is in the pattern of the grains!

DESPAIR. Look at me!

OLD MAN. Look instead at your hands. They are your history. They are the gifts of seven hundred generations of love-making. These shapes, through those hands, came from Egypt, Africa, the Tigris and Euphrates plains to th'Aegean world through Levantine coasts to many-layered magical Troy, to Lemnos, th'Aegean isle, Lesbos, through the Danube corridor, God's bowling alley to Europe.

JOGOT. Look how the dirt yields to my touch! Here's lapis lazuli, magic, and amber!

OLD MAN. These are the gifts of all women and all men of all times to you. Don't look at her. Her morbidity has no memory.

DESPAIR. I must be supported by the adoring gaze of men and women.

TILBURY. Tell us. We don't know.

JOGOT. No one ever told us.

TILBURY. We've had to figure everything out for ourselves.

JOGOT. You see, our culture is dead.

OLD MAN. The deepest mystery is the shape of woman, here, the one who bears and is borne. Around her, here, are encoded the lost rituals and the naive poetry of power that fell brightly from the air of prehistory. This piece of trash is the only record! Without this you have no history and are not human!

DESPAIR. There are no women! Women are only dreamt of!

TILBURY. (*Deep power; partial vision.*) No. That's not true. I once saw the Dakota sun glow on the throat of Tuli Latum.

DESPAIR. (*Beginning to rip off her clothes.*) It's excruciating if you take your eyes off me! Look at my lovely dead eyes and my dead modern thighs! Look, won't you look, at my fine merchandise. I am *available!*

OLD MAN. She looks like a woman, but a woman is tempestuous, sexual, virginal, nourishing, ecstatic, wise and wild. This is a whore—lumpish, drying, boring, dumb and tame. You have unwisely worshipped her.

DESPAIR. Come to me. I am the center of your century.

OLD MAN. Take this. (*Gives the piece of clay.*) You are the carriers now. Go find this woman Tuli. She has eyes like wingbeats. If you can find her, you will also find a wonderful child floating miraculous on the sea at midnight.

JOGOT. There is a child in Tuli Latum.

TILBURY. I want that child.

(DESPAIR *writhes to the floor of the cave and expires, legs awkwardly apart.*)

OLD MAN. (*His life ebbing after his effort.*) I waited for you. Look!

(*LIGHTS come up to reveal* DEMON IDEOLOGY, *seated on a throne on a dais. It is crowned with a grotesque wreath of intertwined human limbs.* IDEOLOGY *wears a bloody shirt and is dressed in texts. Corpses piled like logs make a fetid stairway to its throne.*)

TILBURY. Europe is a graveyard!

JOGOT. All history has sent its rotting tribute down!

OLD MAN. This is the unbeatable demon Ideology, who can make men kill for prophecy, kill their own hands, for the sake of a corpse-cough of philosophy. He kills the Irish and the Jew. He kills the me and the you. He kills the women and the men. He kills the now and the then. He will not listen. He's eaten the alphabet.

JOGOT. The whole alphabet he's eaten?

TILBURY. How do we destroy it?

OLD MAN. I know of no way. Escape. You are the carriers now. (*The* OLD MAN *collapses.* IDEOLOGY *turns slowly about to confront the two men.*)

TILBURY. We're in for it now. No one can stop Ideology. What is it wearing?

JOGOT. A bloody shirt. It's dressed in texts.

TILBURY. (*Drawing his gun and inspecting its chamber.*) Yep. One.

JOGOT. (*Offhand.*) Tell me, that bullet isn't by any chance silver, is it?

TILBURY. No.

JOGOT. Bronze? Brass? Titanium? No special properties whatsoever?

TILBURY. No.

JOGOT. Was it ever blessed, cursed, or cited for heroism?

TILBURY. Nope.

JOGOT. (*Slightly crestfallen; he had expected more.*) Just . . . a bullet.

TILBURY. Just a plain old bullet.

JOGOT. Not even a name.

TILBURY. Nope. Just dead lead.

(IDEOLOGY *begins to make threatening motions.*)

JOGOT. (*Putting his hand on* TILBURY'S *shoulder.*) I don't think you should go against this one. (TILBURY *presses on, impelled by his chest.* TILBURY *faces* IDEOLOGY. *The demon is silent.*) Don't miss.

TILBURY. I don't miss. (*To* IDEOLOGY.) Well, as I was just saying to your colleague there, I am Tilbury—

(*A blinding flash of LIGHT emanates from* IDEOLOGY *and slices through* TILBURY'S *body.* TILBURY *falls to the ground, annihilated.* JOGOT *rises to his feet in disbelief. He goes to* TILBURY.)

JOGOT. (*Cradling* TILBURY's *head.*) Speak, man!

TILBURY. Sorry. He got me good. (*Hands the revolver to* JOGOT.) He doesn't listen at all, so don't bandy words. He's inexplicable fast, so have your gun drawn. He's accurate, too, so make yourself small. He ducks to the side, so slant your shot in. He's tall where he sits, so go down on one knee. Get yourself straight, 'cause he turns things around. (TILBURY *ebbs.*) Good luck, old buddy. I didn't see my vision. (TILBURY's *head sags to one side.* JOGOT *lays* TILBURY's *head down and gets to his feet. He holds the revolver gingerly, awkwardly, as if afraid of it. Amazed and wounded to the heart,* INSPECTOR JOGOT *advances on the last* DEMON *of Hell.*)

JOGOT. Unfair. A full-grown demon matched with an imbecile. (*Keeps advancing, his steps heavy with responsibility.*) The old man dead. Wonderfully resourceful Tilbury gone. Those girls mutilated. But I'm a fool. He's inexplicable fast, so don't bandy words. (*Points the revolver.*) He's as accurate as hell, so duck to the left. No! I've got it wrong. He's bandy-legged and slant, so turn to the right. (*Contorts his body in an attempt to conform to what he remembers of* TILBURY's *instructions.*) He's skewed to the side, so walk with a stoop. (*Becomes more and more contorted; his arms and legs begin to get tangled.*) Turn around first and shoot at a duck. (JOGOT *is reduced to a helpless tangle in front of the all-powerful and imperturbable* DEMON, *each wrist somehow locked in the opposite knee-pit. He holds the unstable position by a great effort. The revolver falls from his hand.* JOGOT *crumples into a heap. Disgusted, he disentangles himself from himself and sits in front of* IDEOLOGY. JOGOT *sobs.*) Couldn't remember a few instructions! Couldn't get out of my own way. How am I going to get out of this century? (*A great cry from the heart.*) Father! Help me! I love thee! (*To* IDEOL-

OGY.) Look, I haven't got a chance of making a that-away. I know I'm a goner. (*The* DEMON *stirs.*) Before you kill me, just let me tell you one thing. I am Jogot, the conscience of Europe. I have discovered hidden guilt in just about every major European capital, and in some of the better suburbs. (*The* DEMON *stirs menacingly;* JOGOT *raises his hand placatingly.*) I know. That's nothing to you. Your strength is that you don't listen. But I am the guilty one. I made you. So . . . (JOGOT *takes his handcuffs out of his pocket and handcuffs his hands together.*) I am going to handcuff myself. I am the criminal. I am a miserable worm. I can't hurt you like this, can I? Go ahead, kill me. But before you do, I want to tell you what the world doesn't know. I am really an artist. (*Confidingly.*) I've had to be secret about my talent because if people knew they would find ways to hurt my feelings. (IDEOLOGY *makes a sound.*) It's nice of you to understand. I've had to hide and protect the poet in Jogot! (*A sound, incomprehensible, from* IDEOLOGY.) Before I die, I want to tell you a story. It's . . . my novel I've been secretly writing. (*A murmur of pleasure from the* DEMON.) Once upon a time . . . (*A gurgle from* IDEOLOGY.) there was a young man, orphaned early, very sensitive and shy, but he wouldn't let the world know it. He loved a princess, who was a captive at a ball both late and masked held by a wealthy ogre who had friends in the military and everything. Sigismondo, enamored of Bellenora, wrote his passion on pieces of paper hidden in coconut husks wrapped in a handkerchief and gave them to a faithful servant who was a simple shepherd but who had been a lowly hermit and was secretly the lost brother of Bellenora who had incensed the duke and angered him by not helping him in his plots to gain rich farmlands, topple the poor but happy king and get Bellenora for himself. Well! —The piece of paper was stolen by a sorcerer who owed a debt to the king. Meanwhile, in a swamp, a little dancing troupe of maidens skilled in the saxophone found the handkerchief. And, Xanthippe had become unwittingly pregnant unknowingly, by sitting on a hot stove—

IDEOLOGY. (*Great voice.*) Who-is-Xanthippe?

JOGOT. (*Casual, flippant, caught up in his tale.*) The low but humble shepherdess violated by the duke's canon, faithful servitor, and secret half-sister to Cleantha of Denmark, whose full sister in turn was eaten by an empty bear. In Sebastopol. In winter. But Sigismondo's best friend in all the world, who had saved at various times the lives of Sigismondo, Sigismondo's mother, father, sister, and pet—

IDEOLOGY. Name of pet, please.

JOGOT. Also fell in love with Bellenora of the white elbows. Think of poor Sigismondo—in a world emptied of meaning, very sensitive, a desk cluttered with unopened mail—in a conflict of love and honor. What could he do but turn to Chloe?

IDEOLOGY. Who-is-Chloe?

JOGOT. A maiden of the Rhine. The unjust accusation of unchasitity—

IDEOLOGY. Unjust?

JOGOT. The lecherous father, the nunnery, the outlaws in the wood, all lead to an escape by means of a leap into the sea, Sigismondo holding her hair in his hand. You see, he had had him woo her through her for him. And against them.

IDEOLOGY. Whom? Him? How? Can a half-sister make an empty bear full? Who was the bear? Why a duke? How come in winter? Shouldn't it be the other way around?

JOGOT. Then the soldiers appeared, pitifully outnumbered. The chase through the Alps, in the pale dawn of longing, the paradoxical situations closing like the massive eyelids of time, the rendezvous at the crimson tree of love, the trenchant ironies, the significant silences, the lonely rooms, the haunted castle, the explicit sex—oh there is so much—but I just want to tell you before you kill me that everything is resolved by a little girl's love for her horse.

IDEOLOGY. (*In thunder.*) *No!*

JOGOT. (*With the insistence which is the infallible mark of literary genius.*) Fully resolved by a little crippled girl's love for her horse and the help—

IDEOLOGY. (*Effort at self-preservation.*) *No! No!*

JOGOT. (*Boring in.*) A little crippled girl's love for her horse and the help of a faithful passenger pigeon. (*Silence.*)

IDEOLOGY. (*Anguished.*) I, Ideology, who have dominated the West by eating history . . . (*He sways.*) and slaughtered hundreds of millions— (*Laughs.*) —with their own hands— (*He sways.*) This imbecile has got past my guard and bored me to death! I knew I should not have listened. (IDEOLOGY *crashes down dead.*)

JOGOT. (*Folding his arms, head erect, mildly.*) You don't have to be rude. (*Then petulantly.*) A lot of thought went into that story. (JOGOT *walks over to* IDEOLOGY, *inspects him, and then turns the carcass over with his foot.* JOGOT *folds his arms and, turning his head, says.*)

JOGOT. Dead. The last demon of hell, Ideology, the unbeatable Ideology, is dead, and I, Jogot, have saved the world. It kind of makes you pause. (JOGOT *walks back to the bodies of the* OLD MAN *and* TILBURY. *He surveys the scene, the bodies everywhere.*) Everything costs. That one could read the history of human aspiration on a piece of trash and . . . (*His voice breaking.*) this one— (JOGOT *kneels beside* TILBURY *and lifts the lifeless body, cradling* TILBURY'S *head.*) was Tilbury, hero. He drove on the great American road, hungry for vision. Honest, courageous, learned, courteous, patient. He knew to beguile Brandywine his guitar of her music. Bitten on the nipple by a child whore, he honored his friends and was honored by them. From all parts of the country—Slack Jackson, Fabled Slade, Speed-Shifter, Backsass, Big Wings Brombeck, Louey the Root, Freshy Bananas, Billy Guillaume, and—Tuli Latum. He saved me in space, and I never thanked him. (*Sobbing.*) Serpents licked his ears at his birth. His hand moved like the rattler striking. He was truly a man. He was truly . . . a hot chocolate!

(*With a great effort,* TILBURY *moves his head.*)

TILBURY. Hot *ticket,* Jogot. How many times do I have to tell you, hot *ticket.*

JOGOT. (*With real joy.*) Tilbury! (*He hugs* TILBURY, *who groans in pain.*) Are you all right?

TILBURY. He got me but he didn't get me good. I think my arm is broken and maybe some ribs—I've got a burning in my gut and no sight in one eye. But I'm alive. He got me but he didn't get me good.

JOGOT. (*Clucking.*) Rest. Soup. (*Becoming tough, competent.*) I've got to get you back to the top.

TILBURY. (*Putting his hand on* JOGOT's *arm.*) What happened to Ideology?

JOGOT. (*A crucial moment in his life.*) I . . . I killed him.

TILBURY. You killed him?

JOGOT. Killed him.

TILBURY. Killed him down dead?

JOGOT. Down. Dead. Gone. Poof.

TILBURY. (*Awed.*) Jogot, I've got to hand it to you. (TILBURY *offers a handshake.*) Shake.

(JOGOT *pushes* TILBURY'S *proffered hand away, feigning business with the handcuffs.*)

JOGOT. You rest. Get these please?

TILBURY. Hey, Jogot, that's a truly great achievement. The old man and the seer both said it couldn't be done. How'd you do it?

JOGOT. Oh, I—

TILBURY. (*Professional interest.*) Karate chop?

JOGOT. Just a small one.

TILBURY. Vital area?

JOGOT. Vital *zone,* really.

TILBURY. Poison vial insinuated? Tap technique?

JOGOT. A very little, actually, of that.

TILBURY. Nose bridge concussion?

JOGOT. Just—the *tip* of the nose. Not really the nose so much—

TILBURY. Last bullet? Fan shot from the hip?

JOGOT. Sort of—yes. Get these, please? (*Gesturing to the cuffs.*)

TILBURY. (*Admiringly as he helps remove the cuffs.*) Great work.

JOGOT. I've got to tell you right away what really happened, *how* I killed Ideology.

TILBURY. Who cares how?

(JOGOT *seizes* TILBURY'S *face by the jaw and forces him to look into his eyes.*)

JOGOT. I didn't kill him by craft or strength—I—bored him to death.

(TILBURY *cocks his head to one side as he realizes what* JOGOT *has said and then explodes in a fit of laughter which hurts but cannot be stopped.* JOGOT *looks hurt and then, seeing from his new perspec-*

tive, begins to laugh, for the first time in his life. Soon he is helpless with laughter, which drains, purges, and strengthens him.)

TILBURY. It took guts to say that, Jogot. Particularly for you.

JOGOT. Why particularly for me?

TILBURY. (*Looking his friend straight in the eye.*) Because you have always been such a jackass.

JOGOT. (*Thinks and instead of retorting, brightens.*) It *did* take guts. Particularly for me. What would have been simple for any honest man was heroic in Jogot! (*Winningly.*) I am basically a very good fellow. I am a jackass and it takes more for a jackass to be heroic. A jackass who has killed the last demon of Hell by boring it to death. A jackass who, if the truth were to be told, has saved the world!

(TILBURY'*s head stiffens. It could be pain, but he manages to convey to* JOGOT *that he is listening intently.*)

TILBURY. Listen.

JOGOT. What do you hear?

TILBURY. The Dakotas. I hear things once whispered in the Dakotas. Tuli whispered things to me in the Dakotas. (TILBURY *is struggling with his breath. In his exultation* JOGOT *does not notice* TILBURY'S *difficulties.*)

JOGOT. (*Serious, ceremonious.*) Tilbury, I believe it only fair to tell you that I mean to be a formidable rival for the hand of Tuli Latum. You may not have noticed it, but I am a very prepossessing young man. When Tuli sees me, her pulses will beat matrimony.

TILBURY. Why then, rivals let us be. When I think of what she said to me one spring evening in Abilene, what she sang to me one night in Cheyenne—

JOGOT. You've never touched her?

TILBURY. Never. But I mean to change that now. I'll fight you every step of the way for Tuli.

JOGOT. (*Serious, martial, extending his hand.*) Done. A rivalry. You are looking at the seven hundred and first generation of love-making.

TILBURY. (*Giving* JOGOT's *hand the downward slap.*) I might as well tell you now, Jogot, there are a couple of things you'll have to do when you get to the United States.

JOGOT. I don't *have* to do anything. I'll seek Tuli in my own way.

TILBURY. (*Taking his book of regulations out of his pocket, reading.*) Says here in my genuine American regulations book that when you go to the States you'll have to go to Oklahoma City and register as an alien. (*A display of ill-controlled anger from* JOGOT.) And it says here—

JOGOT. I don't care *what* it says there!

TILBURY. (*Droning on.*) Says here you have to have your hair cut U.S. American regulation length—

JOGOT. Damn!

TILBURY. Says here you got to think U.S. American thoughts, abstract or otherwise—

JOGOT. Double damn!

TILBURY. (*Climaxing.*) *And* it says here—

JOGOT. What are you reading up at me those regulations you know I can't stand to be read up at from out of for?!

TILBURY. (*Insistently.*) Says here you got to do all these things and then go register as a radical democrat!

JOGOT. (*Exploding.*) Never! I won't! I am Jogot! The conscience of Europe! (JOGOT *stamps his foot and then realizes what he has done.*)

JOGOT. Oh.

TILBURY. (*Smiling.*) Good for you. Get going, Jogot. You can just make the early morning earthquake. (*Rocks and dust begin to fall.*)

JOGOT. (*Looking up.*) Rockfall! Maybe a shaft will open up!

TILBURY. (*Calmly.*) It's your only chance. (*More rocks. Noise.*)

JOGOT. *My* only chance? We're going up together.

TILBURY. (*Casually.*) I don't know. I didn't want to dampen the conversation, but I seem to be dying.

JOGOT. You can't die! I've so much to tell you! I haven't even thanked you for saving my life. I won't let you die! (*Looks up.*) Look! Debris is falling from directly overhead! If that continues there'll be a shaft straight up!

TILBURY. (*Drawling slightly.*) Waal, I wont to get up there but for some doggone reason I cain't *move.* (*More debris showers down.*) You better get a move on or you'll miss your catastrophe.

JOGOT. (*Calm, masterful.*) You don't understand, hombre. We've killed the demons blocking the energy. It's beginning to flow. Soon it will fill you. I'll get you started. (JOGOT *snatches the backpack, and effortlessly picks* TILBURY *up.*) There ain't no grave gonna keep your body down. Not while Jogot is your friend. (JOGOT *begins to climb, easily hefting* TILBURY'S *powerful frame. Up the Upstage rake go the two* FIGURES, *while rocks and dust rain and hail around them.*)

TILBURY. Wait! (*Jogovian.*) I refuse to be saved by someone who does not know my first name!

JOGOT. Oh, for heaven's sake! What is it?

TILBURY. Ask nice. (*Rocks, uproar, explosions.*)

JOGOT. What is your bleeding first name, Mr. Tilbury?

TILBURY. Wilbur.

JOGOT. Wilbur.

TILBURY. Okay. (*Coughs.*) Proceed with saving me. (JOGOT *climbs,* TILBURY *weakens.*) I see something.

JOGOT. Where?

TILBURY. Jogot, are you there?

JOGOT. (*With a touch of desperation he cannot quite entirely suppress.*) I'm holding you. I'm holding you, Wilbur.

TILBURY. Ah yes. I feel you holding me. But I've got to tell you what I'm seeing. It's—a vision! Of wild horses galloping on the Great Plains. And I understand it. Each horse, Jogot, is a nation. I'M SEEING A VISION OF A NOBLE RACE OF NATIONS. Wild horses on a plain, all noble and all free.

JOGOT. Come, Wilbur. I'm going to carry you right out of this century, into a new millennium. Think of Tuli! Think of things whispered in the Dakotas!

(*Drumbeat begins.*)

TILBURY. I am. (*With his old energy.*) Sunsets are beautiful. But sunsets, Jogot, are nothing compared with one Tuli Latum, Route Sixty-six, U.S.A.

JOGOT. (*Excited, gaining altitude.*) We'll put a giant shoulder to history.

TILBURY. Okay, we'll give it a little push.

(*The drumbeat becomes tremendous, pulsating, faster and faster. Suddenly there is a great apocalyptic roar. Tons of debris fall. A flood of light pours down the shaft.*)

TILBURY. Jogot! I see light!

JOGOT. (*Fiercely determined.*) You betchum! Up you go! (JOGOT *gives a mighty heave and in so doing, rips* TILBURY'S *shirt, revealing a large birthmark on his right shoulder. Neither man is aware of it.*)

TILBURY. It's Saturday morning! We did it in half a day! (*A tremendous cock crow, amplified, from the great father of crowing cocks.*) I see the cock, the good bird of dust and daybreak. There he is, a comma in the dawn!

JOGOT. What's up there?

TILBURY. The future, Jogot. Come.

(*The cock crows. Drums to a climax, a blinding LIGHT, and we see the climbing* FIGURES *silhouetted against the dawn. A fabulous release of energy.*)

THE END

PROPERTY PLOT

ACT ONE

Scene 1:

On desk.

- red telephone
- ivory telephone

Personals:

TILBURY

- khaki (not olive) backpack, containing:
  - parachute harness
  - parachute silk (optional)
  - first-aid kit, containing:
    - antiseptic
    - gauze
    - tape
  - cowboy vest
  - cowboy hat
    - (the first-aid kit, the vest and the hat may be loaded in before Scene 5)

TILBURY

- sheet of paper (orders)

JOGOT

- sheet of paper (orders)

TILBURY

- wallet, containing:
  - money

JOGOT

- wallet, containing:
  - identification as police

TILBURY

- regulations book, 3″ x 5″

JOGOT

- airplane ticket

Scene 2:

On metal detector.

telephone

Personals:

TILBURY

khaki backpack

MAN

pistol

MAN

attaché case

CITY PLANNER

brown paper bag, containing:

brick (must read like an unusual piece of construction material; perhaps a sparkling, faceted chunk of clear plastic or a prism)

Scene 3:

Personals:

TILBURY

khaki backpack, now containing:

brick

items listed above

MAN

newspaper

Scene 4:

TILBURY

khaki backpack

Scene 5:

Settled gracefully over TILBURY and JOGOT.

parachute silk

Personals:

WAITER

2 cups of hot chocolate

WAITER
  large napkin
TILBURY
  khaki backpack, containing:
    first-aid kit, containing:
      antiseptic
      gauze
      tape
    cowboy vest
    cowboy hat
TILBURY
  blood capsules (optional)
OLD MAN IN THE TREE
  newspaper
OLD MAN IN THE TREE
  pot (must read as very valuable, exquisite, light-reflecting)
GIRL
  club

ACT TWO

Scene 1:
Leaning against an arch.
  jackhammer (pull-start type, nonfunctional)
Personals:
TILBURY
  tear-away patch on shirt
TILBURY
  regulations book, 3″ x 5″
TILBURY
  khaki backpack, containing:
    pair of boots
    pot
    flashlight

spark plug
plug wrench
gunbelt
holster
six-shooter

JOGOT
key to handcuffs

JOGOT
handcuffs

TILBURY
spare key to handcuffs

TILBURY
head bandage

Scene 4:

Personals:

OLD MAN IN THE UNDERWORLD
fragment of a pot (must read as a marvel; perhaps prismatic)

DESPAIR
sunglasses (optional)

SCENE DESIGN

THE TROUBLE WITH EUROPE

ACT ONE

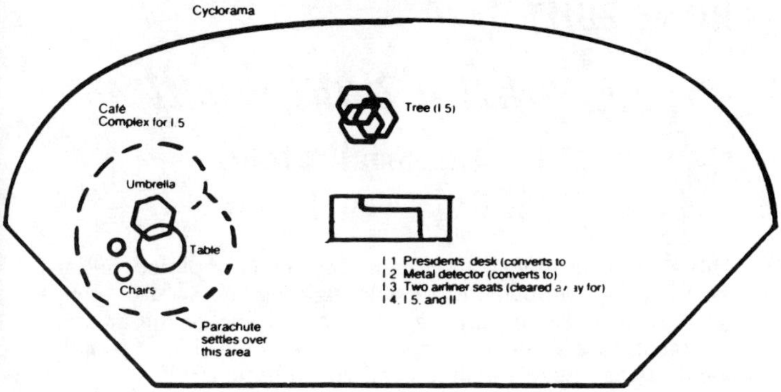

ACT TWO

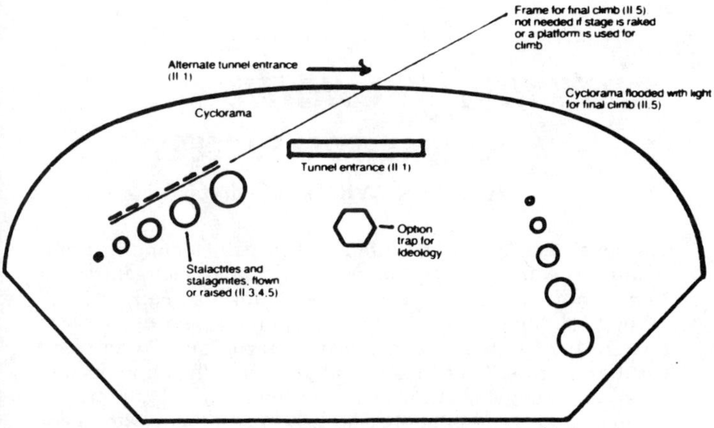